Pro RESTful APIs with Micronaut

Build Java-Based Microservices with REST, JSON, and XML

Second Edition

Sanjay Patni

Apress®

Pro RESTful APIs with Micronaut: Build Java-Based Microservices with REST, JSON, and XML

Sanjay Patni
Santa Clara, CA, USA

ISBN-13 (pbk): 978-1-4842-9199-3   ISBN-13 (electronic): 978-1-4842-9200-6
https://doi.org/10.1007/978-1-4842-9200-6

Copyright © 2023 by Sanjay Patni

Managing Director, Apress Media LLC: Welmoed Spahr
Acquisitions Editor: Susan McDermott
Development Editor: Laura Berendson
Coordinating Editor: Jessica Vakili

Distributed to the book trade worldwide by Springer Science+Business Media New York, 233 Spring Street, 6th Floor, New York, NY 10013. Phone 1-800-SPRINGER, fax (201) 348-4505, e-mail orders-ny@springer-sbm.com, or visit www.springeronline.com. Apress Media, LLC is a California LLC and the sole member (owner) is Springer Science + Business Media Finance Inc (SSBM Finance Inc). SSBM Finance Inc is a **Delaware** corporation.

For information on translations, please e-mail booktranslations@springernature.com; for reprint, paperback, or audio rights, please e-mail bookpermissions@springernature.com.

Apress titles may be purchased in bulk for academic, corporate, or promotional use. eBook versions and licenses are also available for most titles. For more information, reference our Print and eBook Bulk Sales web page at http://www.apress.com/bulk-sales.

Any source code or other supplementary material referenced by the author in this book is available to readers on the Github repository: https://github.com/Apress/*Pro-RESTful-APIs-with-Micronaut*. For more detailed information, please visit http://www.apress.com/source-code.

Printed on acid-free paper

I would like to thank everyone at Apress who I've worked closely with. Thanks to the reviewers; their in-depth reviews helped the quality of the book. A heartfelt thanks goes to my wife, Veena, for her tireless and unconditional support that helped me work on this book. A huge thanks goes to my father, Ajit Kumar Patni, and my mother, Late Basantidevi, for their selfless support that helped me reach where I am today.

Table of Contents

About the Author

Sanjay Patni is a results-focused technologist with extensive experience in aligning innovative technology solutions with business needs to optimize manual steps in the business processes and improving operational efficiency.

At Oracle, he has worked with the Fusion Apps Product development team, where he has identified opportunities for automation of programs related to Fusion Apps codeline management. This involved delivery of GA releases for patching, as well as codelines for ongoing demo, development, and testing. He conceptualized and developed self-service UX for codeline requests and auditing, reducing manual steps by 80%. He also rolled out 12 sprints of codeline creation, automating about 100+ manual steps involving integration with other subsystems using technologies like automation workflow and RESTful APIs.

Prior to joining Oracle, he spent 15+ years in the software industry, defining and delivering key initiatives across different industry sectors. His responsibilities included innovation, requirement, analysis, technical architecture, design, and agile software development of web-based enterprise products and solutions. He pioneered innovative usage of Java in building business applications and received an award from Sun Microsystems. This helped improve feedback for Java APIs for Enterprise in building business application software using Java. He has diverse experience in Application Architecture to include UX, Distributed Systems, Cloud and DevOps.

He has worked as a visiting technical instructor or mentor and conducted classes or training on RESTful APIs design and integration.

He has a strong educational background in computer science with a master's from IIT, Roorkee, India.

About the Technical Reviewer

Massimo Nardone has more than 22 years of experience in security, web and mobile development, cloud, and IT architecture. His true IT passions are security and Android.

He has been programming and teaching how to program with Android, Perl, PHP, Java, VB, Python, C/C++, and MySQL for more than 20 years.

He holds a master of science degree in computing science from the University of Salerno, Italy.

He has worked as a project manager, software engineer, research engineer, chief security architect, information security manager, PCI/SCADA auditor, and senior lead IT security/cloud/SCADA architect for many years.

His technical skills include security, Android, cloud, Java, MySQL, Drupal, Cobol, Perl, web and mobile development, MongoDB, D3, Joomla, Couchbase, C/C++, WebGL, Python, Pro Rails, Django CMS, Jekyll, Scratch, etc.

He currently works as Chief Information Security Officer (CISO) for Cargotec Oyj.

He worked as visiting lecturer and supervisor for exercises at the Networking Laboratory of the Helsinki University of Technology (Aalto University). He holds four international patents (PKI, SIP, SAML, and Proxy areas).

Massimo has reviewed more than 40 IT books for different publishing companies, and he is the coauthor of *Pro Android Games* (Apress, 2015).

Introduction

Databases, websites, and business applications need to exchange data. This is accomplished by defining standard data formats such as Extensible Markup Language (XML) or JavaScript Object Notation (JSON), as well as transfer protocols or web services such as the Simple Object Access Protocol (SOAP) or the more popular Representational State Transfer (REST). Developers often have to design their own Application Programming Interfaces (APIs) to make applications work while integrating specific business logic around operating systems or servers. This book introduces these concepts with a focus on the RESTful APIs.

This book introduces the data exchange mechanism and common data formats. For web exchange, you will learn the HTTP protocol, including how to use XML. This book compares SOAP and REST and then covers the concepts of stateless transfer. It introduces software API design and best design practices. The second half of the book focuses on RESTful APIs design and implementations that follow the Micronaut and Java API for RESTful Web Services. You will learn how to build and consume Micronaut services using JSON and XML and integrate RESTful APIs with different data sources like relational databases and NoSQL databases through hands-on exercises. You will apply these best practices to complete a design review of publicly available APIs with a small-scale software system in order to design and implement RESTful APIs.

This book is intended for software developers who use data in projects. It is also useful for data professionals who need to understand the methods of data exchange and how to interact with business applications. Java programming experience is required for the exercises.

Topics include

- Data exchange and web services

- SOAP vs. REST, state vs. stateless

- XML vs. JSON

- Introduction to API design: REST and Micronaut

- API design practices

- Designing RESTful APIs

- Building RESTful APIs

- Interacting with RDBMS (MySQL)

- Consuming RESTful APIs (i.e., JSON, XML)

CHAPTER 1

Fundamentals of RESTful APIs

Abstract

APIs are not new. They've served as interfaces that enable applications to communicate with each other for decades. But the role of APIs has changed dramatically in the last few years. Innovative companies have discovered that APIs can be used as an interface to the business, allowing them to monetize digital assets, extend their value proposition with partner-delivered capabilities, and connect to customers across channels and devices. When you create an API, you are allowing others within or outside of your organization to make use of your service or product to create new applications, attract customers, or expand their business. Internal APIs enhance the productivity of development teams by maximizing reusability and enforcing consistency in new applications. Public APIs can add value to your business by allowing third-party developers to enhance your services or bring their customers to you. As developers find new applications for your services and data, a network effect occurs, delivering significant bottom-line business impact. For example, Expedia opened up their travel booking services to partners through an API to launch the Expedia Affiliate Network, building a new revenue stream that now contributes $2B in annual revenue. Salesforce

© Sanjay Patni 2023
S. Patni, *Pro RESTful APIs with Micronaut*, https://doi.org/10.1007/978-1-4842-9200-6_1

released APIs to enable partners to extend the capabilities of their platform and now generates half of their annual revenue through those APIs, which could be SOAP based (JAX-WS) and, more recently, RESTful (JAX-RS), Spring Boot, and now Micronaut.

A SOAP web service depends upon a number of technologies (such as UDDI, WSDL, SOAP, HTTP) and protocols to transport and transform data between a service provider and the consumer and can be created with JAX-WS.

Later, Roy Fielding (in the year 2000) presented his doctoral dissertation, "Architectural Styles and the Design of Network-based Software Architecture." He coined the term "REST," an architectural style for distributed hypermedia systems. Put simply, REST (short for REpresentational State Transfer) is an architectural style defined to help create and organize distributed systems. The keyword from that definition should be "style," because an important aspect of REST (and which is one of the main reasons books like this one exist) is that it is an architectural style—not a guideline, not a standard, or anything that would imply that there are a set of hard rules to follow in order to end up having a RESTful architecture.

In this chapter, I'll be covering REST fundamentals, SOAP vs. REST, and web architectural style to provide a solid foundation and better prepare you for what you'll see in later chapters.

The main idea behind REST is that a distributed system, organized RESTfully, will improve in the following areas:

- Performance: The communication style proposed by REST is meant to be efficient and simple, allowing a performance boost on systems that adopt it.

- Scalability of component interaction: Any distributed system should be able to handle this aspect well enough, and the simple interaction proposed by REST greatly allows for this.

- Simplicity of interface: A simple interface allows for simpler interactions between systems, which in turn can grant benefits like the ones previously mentioned.

- Modifiability of components: The distributed nature of the system, and the separation of concerns proposed by REST (more on this in a bit), allows for components to be modified independently of each other at a minimum cost and risk.

- Portability: REST is technology and language agnostic, meaning that it can be implemented and consumed by any type of technology (there are some constraints that I'll go over in a bit, but no specific technology is enforced).

- Reliability: The stateless constraint proposed by REST (more on this later) allows for the easier recovery of a system after failure.

- Visibility: Again, the stateless constraint proposed has the added full state of said request (this will become clear once I talk about the constraints in a bit). From this list, some direct benefits can be extrapolated. A component-centric design allows you to make systems that are very fault tolerant. Having the failure of one component not affect the entire stability of the system is a great benefit for any system. Interconnecting components is quite easy, minimizing the risks when adding new features or scaling up or down. A system designed with REST in mind will be accessible to a wider audience, thanks to its portability (as described earlier). With a generic interface, the system can be used by a wider range of developers. In order to achieve these properties and benefits, a set of constraints were added to REST to help define a uniform connector interface. REST is not suggested to use when you need to enforce a strict contract between a client and a server and when performing transactions that involve multiple calls.

SOAP vs. REST

Table 1-1 has a comparison between SOAP and REST with an example of use cases each can support.

Table 1-1. *SOAP vs. REST comparison*

Topic	SOAP	REST
Origin	SOAP (Simple Object Access Protocol) was created in 1998 by Dave Winer et al. in collaboration with Microsoft. Developed by a large software company, this protocol addresses the goal of addressing the needs of the enterprise market	REST (Representational State Transfer) was created in 2000 by Roy Fielding at UC, Irvine. Developed in an academic environment, this protocol embraces the philosophy of the open Web
Basic Concept	Makes data available as services (verb + noun), for example, "getUser" or "PayInvoice"	Makes data available as resources (nouns), for example, "user" or "invoice"
Pros	Follows a formal enterprise approach Works on top of any communication protocol, even asynchronously Information about objects is communicated to clients Security and authorization are part of the protocol Can be fully described using WSDL	Follows the philosophy of the open Web Relatively easy to implement and maintain Clearly separates client and server implementations Communication isn't controlled by a single entity Information can be stored by the client to prevent multiple calls Can return data in multiple formats (JSON, XML, etc.)
Cons	Spends a lot of bandwidth communicating metadata Hard to implement and is unpopular among web and mobile developers	Only works on top of the HTTP protocol Hard to enforce authorization and security on top of it

(continued)

Table 1-1. (*continued*)

Topic	SOAP	REST
When to use	When clients need to have access to objects available on servers	When clients and servers operate on a web environment
	When you want to enforce a formal contract between a client and a server	When information about objects doesn't need to be communicated to the client
When not to use	When you want the majority of developers to easily use your API	When you need to enforce a strict contract between a client and a server
	When your bandwidth is very limited	When performing transactions that involve multiple calls
Use cases	Financial services	Social media services
	Payment gateways	Social networks
	Telecommunication services	Web chat services
		Mobile services
Examples	`www.salesforce.com/developer/docs/api/—` Salesforce SOAP API	`https://dev.twitter.com/`
Conclusion	Use SOAP if you are dealing with transactional operations and you already have an audience that is satisfied with this technology	Use REST if you're focused on wide-scale API adoption or if your API is targeted at mobile apps

Web Architectural Style

According to Fielding, there are two ways to define a system:

- One is to start from a blank slate—an empty whiteboard—with no initial knowledge of the system being built or the use of familiar components until the needs are satisfied.

- A second approach is to start with the full set of needs for the system, and constraints are added to individual components until the forces that influence the system are able to interact in harmony with each other.

REST follows the second approach. In order to define a REST architecture, a null state is initially defined—a system that has no constraints whatsoever and where component differentiation is nothing but a myth—and constraints are added one by one. The following subsections cover web architectural style constraints. Each of these constraints defines how the framework for RESTful APIs should be architected and designed. Security is another aspect which needs to be considered independently as part of this framework when rolling out RESTful APIs to the end users.

Client-Server

The separation of concerns is the core theme of the Web's client-server constraints.

The Web is a client-server-based system, in which clients and servers have distinct parts to play.

They may be implemented and deployed independently, using any language or technology, so long as they conform to the Web's uniform interface.

Uniform Resource Interface

The interactions between the Web's components—meaning its clients, servers, and network-based intermediaries—depend on the uniformity of their interfaces.

Web components interoperate consistently within the uniform interface's four constraints, which Fielding identified as

- Identification of resources

- Manipulation of resources through representations

- Self-descriptive messages

- Hypermedia as the engine of application state (HATEOAS)

Layered System

Generally speaking, a network-based intermediary will intercept client-server communication for a specific purpose.

Network-based intermediaries are commonly used for enforcement of security, response caching, and load balancing.

The layered system constraints enable network-based intermediaries such as proxies and gateways to be transparently deployed between a client and a server using the Web's uniform interface.

Caching

Caching is one of web architecture's most important constraints. The cache constraints instruct a web server to declare the cache ability of each response's data.

Caching response data can help to reduce client-perceived latency, increase the overall availability and reliability of an application, and control a web server's load. In a word, caching reduces the overall cost of the Web.

Stateless

The stateless constraint dictates that a web server is not required to memorize the state of its client applications. As a result, each client must include all of the contextual information that it considers relevant in each interaction with the web server.

Web servers ask clients to manage the complexity of communicating their application state so that the web server can service a much larger number of clients. This trade-off is a key contributor to the scalability of the Web's architectural style.

Code on Demand

The Web makes heavy use of code on demand, a constraint which enables web servers to temporarily transfer executable programs, such as scripts or plug-ins, to clients.

Code on demand tends to establish a technology coupling between web servers and their clients, since the client must be able to understand and execute the code that it downloads on demand from the server. For this reason, code on demand is the only constraint of the Web's architectural style that is considered optional.

HATEOAS

The final principle of REST is the idea of using hypermedia as the engine of application state (HATEOAS). When developing a client-server solution using HATEOAS, the logic on the server side might change independently of the clients.

Hypermedia is a document-centric approach with the added support for embedding links to other services and information within the document format.

One of the uses of hypermedia and hyperlinks is composing complex sets of information from disparate sources. The information could be within a company private cloud or within a public cloud from disparate sources.

Example:

```
<podcast id="111">
  <customer>http://customers.myintranet.com/customers/1</
customers>
  <link>http://podcast.com/myfirstpodcast</link>
  <description> This is my first podcast </description>
</podcast>
```

Each of these web architecture styles adds beneficial properties to the web system.

By adopting these constraints, teams can build simple, visible, usable, accessible, evolvable, flexible, maintainable, reliable, scalable, and performant systems as shown in Table 1-2.

Table 1-2. *Constraint and system property*

By Following the Constraint	Gain the Following System Property
Client-server interactions	Simple, evolvable, scalable
Stateless communications	Simple, visible, maintainable, evolvable, and reliable
Cacheable data	Visible, scalable, and performant
Uniform interfaces	Simple, usable, visible, accessible, evolvable, and reliable
Layered system	Flexible, scalable, reliable, and performant
Code on demand	Evolvable

Note   I have not covered security in this book as part of REST fundamentals, but security is very important for rolling out RESTful APIs.

What Is REST?

We have briefly introduced REST with REST API fundamentals in the previous section. This section has further introductory details about REST concepts.

"REST" was coined by Roy Fielding in his Ph.D. dissertation to describe a design pattern for implementing networked systems. REST is Representational State Transfer, an architectural style for designing distributed systems. It's not a standard, but rather a set of constraints. It's not tied to HTTP, but is associated most commonly with it.

REST Basics

Unlike SOAP and XML-RPC, REST does not really require a new message format. The HTTP API is CRUD (Create, Retrieve, Update, and Delete):

- GET = "give me some info" (Retrieve)

- POST = "here's some update info" (Update)

- PUT = "here's some new info" (Create)

- DELETE = "delete some info" (Delete)

- And more....

- PATCH = The HTTP method PATCH can be used to update partial resources. For instance, when you only need to update one field of the resource, PUTting a complete resource representation might be cumbersome and utilizes more bandwidth.

- HEAD = The **HEAD** method is identical to the GET method, except that the server must not return a message body in the response. This method is often used for testing hypertext links for validity, accessibility, and recent modification.

- OPTIONS = This method allows the client to determine the options and/or requirements associated with a resource or the capabilities of a server, without implying a resource action or initiating a resource retrieval.

- Notion of "idempotency": The idea that when sending a GET, DELETE, or PUT to the system, the effect should be the same whether the command is sent one or more times, but POST creates an entity in the collection and therefore is not idempotent.

REST Fundamentals

Just to remind you, about 8356 APIs were written in REST by ProgrammableWeb.com in 2016. REST is a resource-based architecture. A resource is accessed via a common interface based on the HTTP standard methods. REST asks developers to use HTTP methods explicitly and in a way that's consistent with the protocol definition. Each resource is identified by a URL. Every resource should support the HTTP common operations, and REST allows that resource to have different representations, for example, text, xml, json, etc. The REST client can ask for a specific representation via the HTTP protocol (content negotiation). Table 1-3 describes data elements used in REST.

Table 1-3. *Structures of REST*

Data Element	Description
Resource	Conceptual target of a hypertext reference, e.g., customer/ order
Resource Identifier	A uniform resource locator (URL) or uniform resource name (URN) identifying a specific resource, e.g., `http://myrest.com/customer/3435`
Resource Metadata	Information describing the resource, e.g., tag, author, source link, alternate location, alias names
Representation	The resource content—JSON Message, HTML Document, JPEG Image
Representation Metadata	Information describing how to process the representation, e.g., media type, last-modified time
Control Data	Information describing how to optimize response processing, e.g., if-modified-since, cache-control-expiry

Let's look at some examples.

Resources

First, here's a REST resource to GET a list of podcasts:

```
http://prorest/podcasts
```

Next, here's a REST resource to GET details of podcast id 1:

```
http://prorest/podcasts/1
```

Representations

Here is an XML representation of a response—GET customer for an id:

```
<Customer>
  <id>123</id>
  <name>John</name>
</Customer>
```

Next, here's a JSON representation of a response—GET customer for an id:

```
{"Customer":{"id":"123","name":"John"}}
```

Content Negotiation

HTTP natively supports a mechanism based on headers to tell the server about the content you expect and you're able to handle. Based on these hints, the server is responsible for returning the corresponding content in the correct format. Figure 1-1 shows an example.

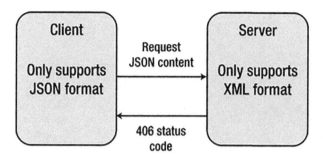

Figure 1-1. *Content negotiation*

If the server doesn't support the requested format, it will send back
a 406 status code (Not Acceptable) to notify the client that made the
request ("The requested resource is only capable of generating content not
acceptable according to the Accept headers sent in the request") according
to the specification.

Summary

REST identifies the key architectural principles of why the Web is prevalent
and scalable. The next step in the education of the Web is to apply these
principles to the semantics Web and the world of web services. REST offers
a simple, interoperable, and flexible way of writing web services that can
be very different than the WS-* that so many of you had training in. In the
next chapter, we will introduce Micronaut—A morder JVM based, full-
stack framework for building modular, easily testable micro service and
server less applications. We will also compare it with similar framework
Spring Boot.

CHAPTER 2

Micronaut

Abstract

Micronaut is a JVM-based modern full-stack microservice framework. This new framework has been developed by the Grails team with an intention to solve problems which have been identified over the years while building the real-world microservices applications.

One of the most exciting features of Micronaut is its compile-time dependency injection mechanism. Most frameworks use reflection and proxies to perform dependency injection at runtime. Micronaut, however, builds its dependency injection data at compile time. The result is faster application startup and smaller memory footprints.

I think it is not an exaggeration if I say we are living in the age of microservices. Microservices became the de facto architecture pattern for every new enterprise-scale application that is being implemented, and many existing monolithic applications are getting migrated into microservices. In the case of the Java world, Spring Boot turned out to be the standard framework to develop microservices. There were some other frameworks like DropWizard, Apache Karaf, and Jersey. But they were not able to give tough competition to Spring Boot, and slowly their usage percentage came down and became insignificant over a period of time. If you observe the evolution of Spring Boot, initially it was not proposed as a microservices solution from Spring. It was initially proposed and implemented as the containerless web application, and the developer community started using it for microservices implementation. But Spring Boot got its own limitations like

- Fixed single language

- Lack of built-in support for data accessing

- Lack of simpler unit testing

- Lack of built-in service discovery

- Lack of built-in load balancing

We need explicit configuration which can be achieved through the cloud services instead of having the built-in support within the framework itself.

Here comes Micronaut which contains the aforementioned built-in features and designed with single and primary intent to serve as the vehicle for microservices development.

Comparison of Micronaut with Spring Boot

Ease of Installation

Both Spring Boot and Micronaut won't be complex for installation and can be installed easily by following the installation instructions. Both frameworks need the following prerequisites:

- A favorite text editor or IDE

- JDK 1.8 or later

- Gradle or Maven latest versions

The code which has been generated through the CLI tool can be directly imported into your IDE:

- Spring Tool Suite (STS): Spring Boot

- Visual Studio Code: Micronaut

Natively Cloud Enabled

When it comes to Spring Boot, to support the previously discussed cloud-specific features, we need to depend on the third-party cloud services or libraries; it doesn't support any of the above-listed features by default, so Micronaut has an advantage here.

The following list of cloud-specific features is directly integrated into the Micronaut runtime:

- Service discovery.

- Eureka, Consul, or ZooKeeper service discovery servers are being supported.

- The Kubernetes container runtime is supported by default.

- Client-side load balancing.

- Netflix Ribbon can be used for load balancing.

- Distributed configuration.

- Distributed tracing.

- Serverless functions.

Serverless Functions

Serverless architecture, where developers will deploy the function. From there onward, they are completely managed by the cloud environment, that is, invocation, execution, and control. But Micronaut's fast startup time, compile-time approach, and low-memory footprint make this framework a great candidate for developing functions, and in fact, Micronaut features have the dedicated support for implementing and deploying functions to the AWS Lambda and any FaaS system that supports running functions as containers.

Application Configuration

Micronaut inspired from both Grails and Spring Boot in integrating configuration properties from different sources directly into the core IoC container. Configurations can be provided by default in either YAML, JSON, Java properties, or Groovy files. The convention is to search for a file called application.yml, application.properties, application.json, or application.groovy.

- Command-line arguments

- Properties from SPRING_APPLICATION_JSON (only if there is any Spring dependency)

- Properties from MICRONAUT_APPLICATION_JSON

- Java system properties

- OS environment variables

- Each environment-specific properties like application-{environment}.{extension} (could be .properties, .json, .yml, or .groovy)

- Application-specific properties from the application.{extension} (could be .properties, .json, .yml, or .groovy)

- Special properties (random values)

Spring Boot supports all the preceding property locations; in addition, it also supports other property locations:

- Spring Boot devtools global settings properties

- @TestPropertySource annotations on your tests

- @SpringBootTest#properties annotation attribute on your tests

- ServletConfig init parameters

- ServletContext init parameters

- JNDI attributes from java:comp/env

- @PropertySource annotations on your @Configuration classes

- Default properties (specified by setting SpringApplication.setDefaultProperties)

"Spring Boot provided more ways to handle with properties when we compared it against Micronaut."

Messaging System Support

Spring Boot supports the integration of external messaging systems, such as

- RabbitMQ

- Apache Kafka

- ActiveMQ

- Artemis

Micronaut also supports the popular messaging systems, such as

- RabbitMQ

- Apache Kafka

"Micronaut has the embedded support for the Apache Kafka." "Both frameworks have the support of the popular messaging systems but Spring Boot supports more tools."

Security

Spring Boot supports the following security mechanisms by default:

- MVC Security
- WebFlux Security
- OAuth2
- Actuator Security

Micronaut supports the following security mechanisms by default:

- Authentication Providers
- Security Rules
- IP Pattern Rule
- Secured Annotation
- Intercept URL Map
- Built-In Endpoints Security
- Authentication Strategies
- Basic Auth
- Session Authentication
- JSON Web Token
- Built-In Security Controllers
- Retrieve the Authenticated User
- Security Events

Caching

Spring Boot supports the following caching providers:

- Redis
- Couchbase
- Generic
- JCache (JSR-107)
- EhCache 2.x
- Hazelcast
- Infinispan
- Caffeine

Micronaut supports the following list of caching providers:

- Caffeine (by default, Micronaut supports it)
- Redis

"Obviously, Spring Boot is leading in supporting caching providers."

Management and Monitoring

Micronaut inspired by the Grails, Spring Boot, and Micronaut management dependency adds support to monitor your applications via endpoints, the special URIs that return details about the state of your application and health:

- Creating endpoints
- Built-in endpoints

API Portfolio

This book will take three business domain problems and build a portfolio of APIs.

Online Flight

To illustrate features of Micronaut, this book will take an example of an "online flight" application. The application will enable passengers to view flight they are traveling. You will define two component classes:

1. A service component that lets a passenger see what flights they are booked in.

2. A repository component that stores passengers for a flight. Initially, you will store passengers in memory for simplicity.

Object	Field	Type
Passenger	Name	String
Flight	Origin	String
	Destination	String
	Departure	Datetime
	Flight#	int

Message

This API will enable sending messages to the users in the system.

Object	Fields	Type
Message	Message	String
	From	String
	To	String
	Creation Date	Date

Quote

To illustrate features of Micronaut data, this book will take an example of an "online quote" application. The application will enable buyers to create and view quotes including products they want to buy. You will define three component classes:

1. Catalog to list products with their price

2. Quote for a customer including line items of the products with total price

3. Quote line item including products with unit price and quantity

Object	Field	Type
Product	Name	String
	Description	String
	Unit Price	Float
Quote	Customer	String
	Quote Date	Date
	Address	Object

Object	Field	Type
	Quote Line	Object
	Total Price	Float
Quote Line	Product	Object
	Quantity	Long
	Unit Price	Float

Software

This book will use the following software for the coding problems.

Micronaut

https://micronaut.io/download/

INSTALLING WITH SDKMAN!

This tool makes installing the Micronaut framework on any Unix-based platform (Mac OSX, Linux, Cygwin, Solaris, or FreeBSD) easy.

Simply open a new terminal and enter

```
$ curl -s https://get.sdkman.io | bash
```

Follow the on-screen instructions to complete installation. Open a new terminal or type the command:

```
$ source "$HOME/.sdkman/bin/sdkman-init.sh"
```

Then install the latest stable version of the framework:

```
$ sdk install micronaut
```

If prompted, make this your default version.

After installation is complete, it can be tested with

```
$ mn --version
```

That's all there is to it!

Now let's create "hello from Micronaut."

It is assumed that micronaut 3, gradle and jdk11 is installed.

mn create-app hello-world

JDK 11

```
https://jdk.java.net/archive/
```

POSTMAN

```
www.postman.com/downloads/
```

CURL

```
https://curl.se/download.html
```

IDE

You have two choices to use the IDE.

Visual Studio Code

```
https://code.visualstudio.com/download
```

IntelliJ

```
www.jetbrains.com/idea/download/
```

Maven

```
https://maven.apache.org/download.cgi
```

Setting Up an IDE

The application created in the previous section contains a "main class" located in src/main/java that looks like the following:

```
package hello.world;
import io.micronaut.runtime.Micronaut;
public class Application {
    public static void main(String[] args) {
        Micronaut.run(Application.class);
    }
}
```

This is the class that is run when running the application via Gradle or via deployment.

Configuring Visual Studio Code

In this book, we will illustrate the use of Visual Studio Code for editing Java code.

Open code created in the hello-world folder by clicking "Open" and navigating to the hello-world folder. Micronaut can be set up within Visual Studio Code. You will need to first install the Java Extension Pack.

6. Visual Studio IntelliCode

Install the Extension Pack for Java

To get started with this extension pack,

Extension Pack for Java is a collection of popular extensions that can help write, test, and debug Java applications in Visual Studio Code. Visual Studio Code support currently only works for Maven builds. The hello world example will run using the command line since it uses gradle.

https://code.visualstudio.com/docs/java/extensions

Once the extension pack is installed, you could use an IDE for editing Java code.

Now create a new class using File ➤ New File ➤ New Java Class and paste

```
package hello.world;
import io.micronaut.http.MediaType;
import io.micronaut.http.annotation.Controller;
import io.micronaut.http.annotation.Get;
@Controller("/hello") public class HelloController {
@Get(produces = MediaType.TEXT_PLAIN)
public String index() {return "Hello from Micronaut"; }
 }
```

Save the file as HelloController.java. Files will look like the preceding example. Now to run from the command prompt

```
cd ~/hello-world
./gradlew run
curl http://localhost:8080/hello
```

You can also run the application from an IDE by selecting Application. java and right-clicking and running.

```
https://walkingtreetech.medium.com/spring-boot-vs-micronaut-
the-battle-unleashed-2682354a88e9
```

Summary

In this chapter, we reviewed features of Micronaut and compared those with Spring Boot. We also analyzed sample domains—flight status message, and quote to create a portfolio of APIs using Micronaut.

CHAPTER 3

Introduction: XML and JSON

Abstract

This chapter introduces basic concepts about XML and JSON. At the end of this chapter, there is an exercise to demonstrate XML and JSON responses from a Micronaut app.

What Is XML?

eXtensible Markup Language (XML) is a text-based markup language which is a standard for data interchange on the Web. As with HTML, you identify data using tags (identifiers enclosed in angle brackets, like this: `<...>`). Collectively, the tags are known as "markup." It puts a label on a piece of data that identifies it (e.g., `<message>...</message>`). In the same way that you define the field names for a data structure, you are free to use any XML tags that make sense for a given application. Naturally, though, for multiple applications to use the same XML data, they have to agree on the tag names they intend to use. Here is an example of some XML data you might use for a messaging application:

```
<message>
<to>you@yourAddress.com</to>
<from>me@myAddress.com</from>
<subject>XML Is Really Cool>
</subject>
<text>
How many ways is XML cool? Let me count the ways...
</text>
</message>
```

Tags can also contain attributes (additional information included as part of the tag itself) within the tag's angle brackets. If you consider the information in question to be part of the essential material that is being expressed or communicated in the XML, put it in an element. For human-readable documents, this generally means the core content that is being communicated to the reader. For machine-oriented record formats, this generally means the data that comes directly from the problem domain. If you consider the information to be peripheral or incidental to the main communication, or purely intended to help applications process the main communication, use attributes. The following example shows an email message structure that uses attributes for the to, from, and subject fields:

```
<message to=you@yourAddress.com from=me@myAddress.com
subject="XML Is Really Cool">
<text>
How many ways is XML cool? Let me count the ways...
</text>
</message>
```

One really big difference between XML and HTML is that an XML document is always constrained to be well formed. There are several rules that determine when a document is well formed, but one of the most important is that every tag has a closing tag. So, in XML, the </to> tag is not optional. The <to> element is never terminated by any tag other than </to>.

Note   Another important aspect of a well-formed document is that all tags are completely nested. So you can have <message>..<to>..</to>..</message>, but never <message>..<to>..</message>..</to>.

An XML Schema is a language for expressing constraints about XML documents. There are several different schema languages in widespread use, but the main ones are Document Type Definitions (DTDs). It defines the legal building blocks of an XML document. It also defines the document structure with a list of legal elements and attributes.

XML Comments

XML comments look just like HTML comments:

```
<message to=you@yourAddress.com from=me@myAddress.com
subject="XML Is Really Cool">
<!-- This is comment -->
<text>
How many ways is XML cool? Let me count the ways...
</text>
</message>
```

To complete this introduction to XML, note that an XML file always starts with a prolog. The minimal prolog contains a declaration that identifies the document as an XML document, like this:

```
<?xml version="1.0"?>
```

The declaration may also contain additional information, like this:

```
<?xml version="1.0" encoding="ISO-8859-1" standalone="yes"?>
```

- version: Identifies the version of the XML markup language used in the data. This attribute is not optional.

- encoding: Identifies the character set used to encode the data. "ISO-8859-1" is "Latin-1," the Western European and English language character set. (The default is compressed Unicode: UTF-8.)

- standalone: Tells whether or not this document references an external entity or an external data type specification. If there are no external references, then "yes" is appropriate.

Why Is XML Important?

It is important because it allows the flexible development of user-defined document types, which means that it provides a persistent, robust, nonproprietary, and verifiable file format which can be used for the storage and transmission of data for both on and off the Web. In addition, XML

- Provides plain text: Plain text makes it readable.

- Provides data identification: By use of tags, data can be identified.

- Provides styleability: Using XSLT (Extensible Stylesheet Language Transformations), data can be made in a presentable form.

- Is easily processed (XML parsers, as well as well-formed parsers).

- Is hierarchical (through nested tags).

How Can You Use XML?

There are several basic ways to make use of XML:

- Document-driven programming, where XML documents are containers that build interfaces and applications from existing components

- Archiving: The foundation for document-driven programming, where the customized version of a component is saved (archived) so it can be used later

- Binding, where the DTD or schema that defines an XML data structure is used to automatically generate a significant portion of the application that will eventually process that data

Pros and Cons of XML

Some of the pros and cons of XML are explained as follows:

- Pros
    - Readable and editable by developers.
    - Error checking by means of schema and DTDs.
    - Can represent complex hierarchies of data.
    - Unicode gives flexibility for international operation.
    - Plenty of tools in all computer languages for both creation and parsing.
- Cons
    - Bulky text with low payload/formatting ratio (but can be compressed).

- Both creation and client-side parsing are CPU intensive.

- Common word processing characters are illegal (MS Word "smart" punctuation, for example).

- Images and other binary data require extra encoding.

What Is JSON?

JSON or JavaScript Object Notation is a lightweight text-based open standard designed for human-readable data interchange. Conventions used by JSON are known to programmers, which include those with knowledge of C, C++, Java, Python, Perl, etc.

- The format was specified by Douglas Crockford.

- It was designed for human-readable data interchange.

- It has been extended from the JavaScript scripting language.

- The filename extension is `.json`.

- The JSON Internet media type is `application/json`.

- JSON is easy to read and write.

- JSON is language independent.

JSON Syntax

In this section, we will discuss what JSON's basic data types are and their syntax. Figure 3-1 shows the basic data types of JSON.

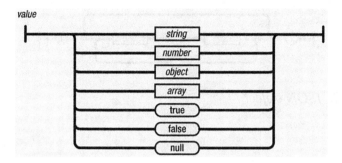

Figure 3-1. *Basic data types*

Strings

Strings are enclosed in double quotes and can contain the usual assortment of escaped characters.

Numbers

Numbers have the usual C/C++/Java syntax, including exponential (E) notation. All numbers are decimal—no octal or hexadecimal.

Objects

An object is an unordered set of a name/value pair. The pairs are enclosed within braces ({ }).

Example:

```
{ "name": "html", "years": 5 }
```

Pairs are separated by commas. There is a colon between the name and the value.

The syntax of a JSON object is shown in Figure 3-2.

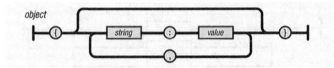

Figure 3-2. *JSON object*

Arrays

An array is an ordered collection of values. The values are enclosed within brackets. The syntax of JSON arrays is shown in Figure 3-3.

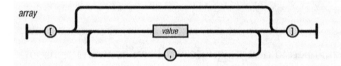

Figure 3-3. *JSON arrays*

Booleans

It can have either true or false values.

Null

The value is that it's empty.

Why Is JSON Important?

There is a reason why JSON is becoming very popular as a data exchange format (more important than it being less verbose than XML): programmers are sick of writing parsers! But "wait," you say. "Surely there are XML parsers available for you to use so that you don't have to roll your own." Yes, there are. But while XML parsers handle the low-level syntactic parsing of XML tags, attributes, etc., you still need to walk the DOM tree or, worse, build one yourself with nothing but a SAX parser (Objective-C iPhone SDK I'm looking at you!). And that code you write will of course depend on whether the XML you need to make sense of looks like this:

```
1 <person first-name="John" last-name="Smith"/>
```

or this:

```
1 <person>
2 <first-name>John</first-name>
3 <last-name>Smith</last-name>
4 </person>
```

or this:

```
1 <object type="Person">
2 <property name="first-name">John</property>
3 <property name="last-name">Smith</property>
4 </object>
```

or any of the myriad of other ways one can conceive of expressing the same concept (and there are many). The standard XML parser does not help you in this regard. You still need to do some work with the parse tree.

Working with JSON is a different, and superior, experience. First, the simpler syntax helps you avoid the need to decide between many different ways of representing your data (as we saw earlier with XML), much less which rope to hang yourself with. Usually, there is only one straightforward way to represent something:

```
1 { "first-name" : "John",
2 "last-name" : "Smith" }
```

How Can You Use JSON?

The following discusses how you can use JSON:

- It is used while writing JavaScript-based applications that include browser extensions and websites.

- JSON format is used for serializing and transmitting structured data over a network connection. It is primarily used to transmit data between a server and web applications.

- Web services and APIs use JSON format to provide public data.

Pros and Cons of JSON

The following are pros and cons of JSON:

Pros

- Easy to read/write/parse

- Reasonably succinct (compared with XML, for instance)

- Common "standard" with many libraries available

Cons

- Not as light as binary formats.

- Can't use comments.

- It's "encapsulated," meaning that you can't readily stream/append data, but have to break it up into individual objects. XML has the same problem, whereas CSV does not.

- Difficult to describe the data you're presenting (easier with XML).

- Unable to enforce, or validate against, a structure/schema.

XML and JSON Comparison

This section compares XML and JSON based upon different properties.

Table 3-1. *XML and JSON comparison*

Property	XML	JSON
Simplicity	XML is simple and human-readable	JSON is much simpler than XML as well as human-readable
Self-Describing	Yes	Yes
Processing	XML is processed easily	JSON is processed more easily because its structure is simpler
Performance	Not optimized for performance due to tags	Faster than XML because of size
Openness	XML is open	JSON is at least as open as XML, perhaps more so because it is not in the center of a corporate/political standardization struggle
Object-Oriented	XML is document oriented	JSON is data oriented. JSON can be mapped more easily to object-oriented systems
Interoperability	XML is interoperable	JSON has the same interoperability potential as XML

(*continued*)

Table 3-1. (*continued*)

Property	XML	JSON
Internationalization	Supports Unicode	Supports Unicode
Extendability	XML is extensible	JSON is not extensible because it does not need to be. JSON is not a document markup language, so it is not necessary to define new tags or attributes to represent data in it
Adoption	XML is widely adopted by the industry	JSON is just beginning to become known. Its simplicity and the ease of converting XML to JSON makes JSON ultimately more adoptable

Implementing APIs to Return XML and JSON Messages

```
https://micronaut.io/launch/
```
As per the screen, select

Application Type: Micronaut Application

Java Version: 11

Name: message

Package: com.rest

Build Tool: maven

Click "Generate Project."

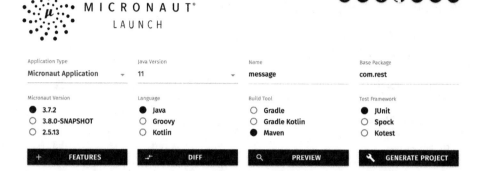

Application Type		Java Version		Name		Base Package	
Micronaut Application	▾	11	▾	message		com.rest	

Micronaut Version	Language	Build Tool	Test Framework
● 3.7.2	● Java	○ Gradle	● JUnit
○ 3.8.0-SNAPSHOT	○ Groovy	○ Gradle Kotlin	○ Spock
○ 2.5.13	○ Kotlin	● Maven	○ Kotest

+ FEATURES	⇆ DIFF	🔍 PREVIEW	🔧 GENERATE PROJECT

New Folder

Name of new folder inside "rest":

model

Cancel   Create

Your Micronaut app is ready for takeoff.

Unix/Linux/macOS   Windows

Unzip the archive

```
unzip message.zip
```

cd into the project

```
cd message
```

Launch!

```
./mvnw mn:run
```

Once you've gotten your new project started, you can continue your journey by reviewing our documentation and learning resources

CLOSE   START OVER

Open message in Visual Source Code.

Now add a new folder model by selecting File ➤ Add new folder and navigating to code generated by Micronaut.

Then create a new domain class Message.

The following code creates a domain object Message with an attribute message. Getter and setter methods are created in the IDE.

```java
package com.rest.model;

import javax.validation.constraints.NotNull;

public class Message {
@NotNull
private String message;
public String getMessage() {
        return message;
}
public void setMessage(String message) {
    this.message = message;
}
}
~
```

Now create a new folder controller after navigating to message code generated by Micronaut.

The following code exposes two endpoints:

    a.   message/xml for getting the message attribute value in XML

    b.   Message/json for getting the message attribute value in JSON format

Create a controller:

```
package com.rest.controllers;
import com.rest.model.Message;
import io.micronaut.http.annotation.Get;
import io.micronaut.http.annotation.Controller;
import io.micronaut.http.HttpResponse;
import io.micronaut.http.MediaType;
import io.micronaut.http.annotation.Produces;

@Controller("/message")  // <2>
public class MessageController {

  @Produces(MediaType.TEXT_XML)
  @Get("/xml")
    public HttpResponse<?> messageXml() {
        Message message = new Message();
        message.setMessage("Hello from Micronaut");
        final String xml = encodeAsXml(message);
        return HttpResponse.ok(xml).contentType(MediaType.
        APPLICATION_XML_TYPE);
    }
  @Produces(MediaType.TEXT_JSON)
  @Get("/json")
    public HttpResponse<?> messageJson() {
        Message message = new Message();
        message.setMessage("Hello from Micronaut");
```

```java
        return HttpResponse.ok(message);
    }

    private String encodeAsXml(final Message message) {
        return String.format("<message>%s</message>", message.
        getMessage());
    }

}
```

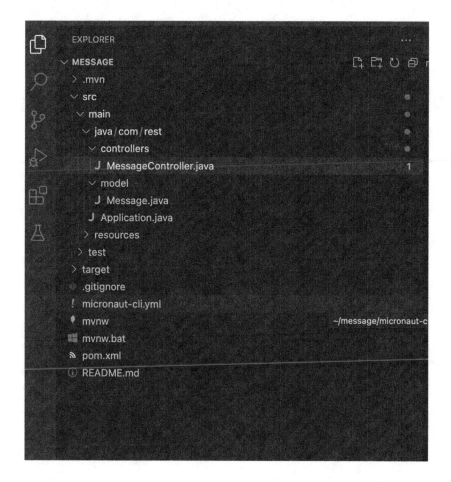

You should have files as shown earlier.

Run the app in the IDE using Run ➤ Run without Debugging.

You could also run in the IDE by selecting Application.java and then right-clicking it.

Using POSTMAN as per the screenshot view JSON and XML response of message

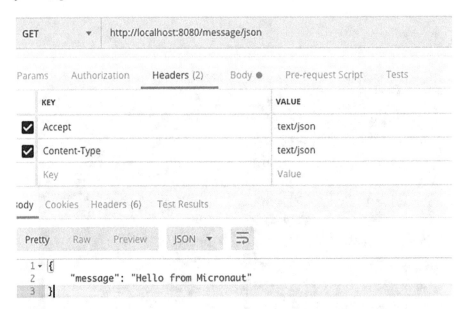

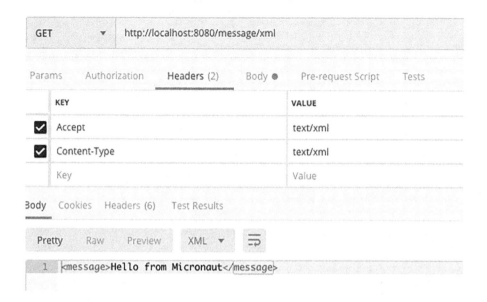

Summary

In this chapter, we reviewed messaging using XML and JSON formats and compared them. Then we developed APIs to return XML and JSON responses from a Micronaut app.

CHAPTER 4

API Design and Modeling

Abstract

This chapter starts with API design strategies and then goes into API creation process and modeling. Best practices for REST API design are discussed, followed by API solution architecture. In the exercises, a simple API is designed for podcast subscription and then modeling using OpenAPI.

API Design Strategies

As the UI is to UX (user experience), the API is to APX (Application Programming Experience). In APX, it is important to answer the following questions:

- What should be exposed?

- What is the best way to expose the data?

- How should the API be adjusted and improved?

In addition, let's discuss why we should develop a nice Application Programming Experience.

© Sanjay Patni 2023
S. Patni, *Pro RESTful APIs with Micronaut*, https://doi.org/10.1007/978-1-4842-9200-6_4

51

A nice API will encourage the developers to use it and share it with others, creating a virtuous cycle where each additional successful implementation leads to more engagement and more contributions from developers who add value to your service. I'll start by saying that API design is hard.

Also, a nice API will help to grow an ecosystem of employees, customers, and partners who can use and help to continue to evolve your API in ways that are mutually beneficial.

There are four strategies for API design:

- Bolt-on strategy: This is when you have an existing application and add an API after the fact. This takes advantage of existing code and systems (Figure 4-1).

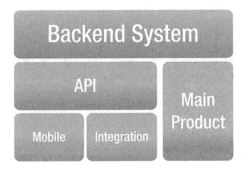

Figure 4-1. *Bolt-on strategy*

- Greenfield strategy: This is the other extreme. This is a strategy behind "API first" or "mobile first" and is the easiest scenario to develop an API. Since you're starting from scratch, you can make use of technologies and concepts that may not have been available before (Figure 4-2).

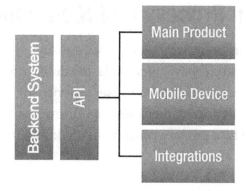

Figure 4-2. *Greenfield strategy*

A greenfield or API-first strategy is a simulation-based design implementation.

The simulation of a back-end system is the development of a back-end system without needing fully implemented back-end systems. With the simulation of APIs, consumers can start the development of apps without fully developed APIs.

- Agile design strategy: Agility is based on the premise that you can start without a full set of specs. You can always adapt and change the specs later, as you go and learn more. Through multiple iterations, architectural design can converge to the right solution. An agile approach should only be applied until the API is published.

- Finally, you have the façade strategy, which is the middle ground between greenfield and bolt-on. In this case, you can take advantage of existing business systems, yet shape them to what you prefer and need. This gives them the ability to keep working systems in place while making the underlying architecture better.

API Creation Process and Methodology

In this section, we are going to review the API creation process and methodology. In order to deliver great APIs, the design must be a first-order concern. Like optimizing for UX (user experience) has become a primary concern in UI development, also optimizing for APX (API user experience) should be a primary concern in API development.

Process

First, determine your business value. When thinking about business value, think of the "elevator pitch" about why you need an API. Developer engagement is not a great goal; you need a tangible goal: increase user engagement, move activity off the main product to the API, engage and retain partners, and so on.

Choose your metrics, for example:

- Number of developer keys in use

- Number of applications developed

- Number of users interacting via the API

- Number of partner integrations

- How the API is enhancing goals of the company as a whole rather than simply determining how many people have begun to integrate

API Methodology

It consists of five phases in the case of the agile strategy:

- Domain analysis or API description

- Architecture design

- Prototyping

- Building an API for production

- Publishing the API

Domain Analysis or API Description

Define your use cases for domain analysis. Who are the participants? Are they external or internal? Which API solutions do consumers want to build with the API? Which other API solutions would be possible with the API?

What would the API that the consumer wants to use look like? What apps does the consumer want to build? What data or domain objects does the consumer want to use in their app?

Break activities into steps or write down the usage scenario:

- A dependent resource cannot exist without another.

  - For example, the association of a podcast and its consumer cannot be determined unless the podcast and its consumer are created.

- An independent resource can exist without another.

  - For example, a podcast resource can exist without any dependency.

- An associative resource exists independently but still has some kind of relation, that is, it may be connected by reference.

  - As mentioned earlier

55

The next step is to identify possible transitions between resource states. Transitions between states provide an indicator of the HTTP method that needs to be supported. For the example of the podcast which could be added to a playlist, let's analyze different states (Table 4-1).

Table 4-1. *Domain analysis example*

State	Operation	Domain Object	Description
CREATE	POST	PODCAST	Creates podcast
READ	GET	PODCAST	Reads podcast
READ	GET/{podcast_id}	PODCAST	Reads podcast
UPDATE	PUT/{playlist_id}	PODCAST	Updates podcast

Also, verify by building a simple demo app. More than curl calls, this demo app provides a showcase for the API and can be reused in later stages.

Architecture Design

In this phase, the API description or analysis phase is further redefined. Architecture design should make decisions about

- Protocol
- Endpoints
- URI design
- Security
- Performance or availability

Detail design description:

- Resources

- Representations

- Content types

- Parameters

- HTTP methods

- HTTP status codes

- Consistent naming

In addition, look into reusability by looking at common APIs in the API portfolio. Design decisions should be consistent with the API in the API portfolio. The API portfolio is a collection of APIs in an enterprise, as discussed in Chapter 5.

As part of the design verification, the demo app can be further extended here with design decisions. Issues to be verified are that

- The API is still easy to use.

- The API is simple and supports use cases.

- The API follows an architectural style.

Prototyping

Prototyping is the preparation for the production implementation. Take complex use cases and implement end to end with high fidelity. The prototype is incomplete and uses shortcuts. It can have a simulation of the API if the back-end functionality is not available at the time of building the prototype. Once the prototype is made, then there is the acceptance test with pilot consumers as verification of the API. Pilot consumers are internal customers from the API provider's team.

Implementation

The implementation needs to conform to the API description and needs to be delivered as soon as possible. In addition, the API is fully integrated into the back-end system and API portfolio. This should have all the desired functionality as well as nonfunctional aspects of the API, like performance, security, and availability. At this stage, the API description should be stable since it has gone through multiple iterations. For verification, handpicked API consumers could be identified at this stage.

Publish

Publishing of the API does not require a lot of work, but this is a big milestone for the API. From an organizational perspective, the responsibility of the API is transferred from development to the operational unit. After publishing, there is no agility in the development process. Any change requires a traditional change management process. As part of the verification, there is analysis on successful vs. failed API calls and documentation gaps which are supported by the maintenance team.

API Modeling

Modeling the schema for your API means creating a design document that can be shared with other teams, customers, or executives. A schema model is a contract between your organization and the clients who will be using it. A schema model is essentially a contract describing what the API is, how it works, and exactly what the endpoints are going to be. Think of it as a map of the API, a user-readable description of each endpoint, which can be used to discuss the API before any code is written. Figure 4-3 shows the API Modeling framework where you have API specifications defined and generate API documentation. Also, generate server and client source code.

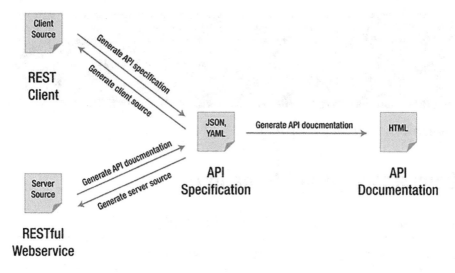

Figure 4-3. *API Modeling*

Creating this model before starting development helps you to ensure that the API you create will meet the needs described by the use cases you've identified. The three schema modeling systems and the markup languages they use are as follows:

- RAML: Markdown, relatively new. Good online modeling tool: RESTful APIs Modeling Language

- OpenAPI (Swagger): JSON, large community

- Blueprint: Markdown, low adoption

The OpenAPI (Swagger) exercise in this chapter shows the modeling done for the podcast resource.

Each of the schema modeling languages has tools available to automate testing or code creation based on the schema model you've created, but even without this functionality, the schema model helps you to have a solid understanding of the API before a single line of code is written.

Figure 4-4 shows the API Modeling tool.

Figure 4-4. *API Modeling tool*

Comparison of API Modeling

Table 4-2. *Comparison of API Modeling tools*

Category	Property	RAML	API Blueprint	Swagger
What is behind name?	Format	YAML	Markdown (MOSN)	JSON
	Available at	GitHub	GitHub	GitHub
	Sponsored by	MuleSoft	Apiary	SmartBear
	Initial Commit	Sep 2013	Apr 2013	Jul 2011
	Commercial Offering	Yes	Yes	Yes
How does it model REST?	Resources	X	X	X ("api")
	Methods/Actions	X ("methods")	X ("actions")	X ("operations")
	Query Parameters	X	X	X

(continued)

Table 4-2. (*continued*)

Category	Property	RAML	API Blueprint	Swagger
	Path/URL Parameters	X	X	X
	Representation	X	X	X
	Header Parameters	X	X	X
	Documentation	X	X	X
	References	http:// raml.org	https:// apiblueprint. org	http:// swagger.io
	Design	API first	Design first	Existing API
	Code Generation	X		X
Who are the customers?				Apigee, Microsoft, PayPal

In summary

- Swagger has a very strong modeling language for defining exactly what's expected of the system—very useful for testing and creating coding stubs for a set of APIs.

- RAML is designed to support a design-first development flow and focuses on consistency.

- API Blueprint is more documentation focused, with user-readable models and documentation as its first priority.

Each project brings different strengths and weaknesses to the table, and in the end, it's really about what strengths you need and which weaknesses you cannot afford. Overall, RAML fared the best in these different categories, and, while the developer community is not as large as the others, I think it's safe to say it will keep growing.

The overall winner is RAML.

Best Practices

REST is an architectural style and not a strict standard; it allows for a lot of flexibility. Because of that flexibility and freedom of structure, there is also a big appetite for design best practices. These best practices are discussed here in this section.

Keep Your Base URL Simple and Intuitive

The base URL is the most important design affordance of your API. A simple and intuitive base URL design makes using your API easy. Affordance is a design property that communicates how something should be used without requiring documentation. A door handle's design should communicate whether you pull or push. For Web API design, there should be only two base URLs per resource. Let's model an API around a simple object or resource (a customer) and create a Web API for it. The first URL is for a collection; the second is for a specific element in the collection:

- `/customers`: Collection

- `/customers/1`: Specific element

Boiling it down to this level will also force the verbs out of your base URLs. Keep verbs out of your URLs as shown in Table 4-3.

Table 4-3. *Nouns and verbs*

Resource	POST Create	GET Read	PUT Update	DELETE Delete
/customers	New customer	List customers	Bulk update	Delete all
/ customers/12	–	Show customer 12	If exists, update If not, error	Delete customer 12

In summary

- Use two base URLs per resource. Keep verbs out of your base URLs. Use HTTP verbs to operate on the collections and elements.

- The level of abstraction depends on your scenario. You also want to expose a manageable number of resources.

    - Aim for concrete naming and to keep the number of resources between 12 and 24.

- An intuitive API uses plural rather than singular nouns and concrete rather than abstract nouns.

- Resources almost always have relationships to other resources. What's a simple way to express these relationships in a Web API? Let's look again at the API we modeled in nouns are good, verbs are bad—the API that interacts with our podcast resource. Remember, we had two base URLs: /podcasts and /podcasts/1234. We're using HTTP verbs to operate on the resources and collections. Our podcasts belong to customers. To get all the podcasts belonging to a specific customer or to create a new podcast for that customer, do a GET or a POST:

63

- GET /customers/5678/podcasts

- POST /customers/5678/podcasts

- Sweep complexity under the "?". Make it simple for developers to use the base URL by putting optional states and attributes behind the HTTP question mark. To get all customers in sfo city of ca state of usa country:

    - GET /customers?country=usa&state=ca&city=so

Error Handling

Many software developers, including myself, don't always like to think about exceptions and error handling, but it is a very important piece of the puzzle for any software developer and especially for API designers. Why is good error design especially important for API designers? From the perspective of the developer consuming your Web API, everything at the other side of that interface is a black box. Errors therefore become a key tool providing context and visibility into how to use an API. First, developers learn to write code through errors. The "test-first" concepts of the extreme programming model and the more recent "test-driven development" models represent a body of best practices that have evolved because this is such an important and natural way for developers to work. Second, in addition to when they're developing their applications, developers depend on well-designed errors at the critical times when they are troubleshooting and resolving issues after the applications they've built using your API are in the hands of their users.

Handling errors: Let's take a look at how three top APIs approach

- Facebook

    HTTP Status Code: 200

    ```
    {"type" : "OauthException", "message":"(#803) Some of
    the aliases you requested do not exist: foo.bar"}
    ```

- Twilio

  HTTP Status Code: 401

  ```
  {"status" : "401", "message":"Authenticate","code":
  20003, "more info": "http://www.twilio.com/docs/
  errors/20003"}
  ```

- Another example of error messaging from SimpleGeo

  HTTP Status Code: 401

  ```
  {"code" : 401, "message": "Authentication Required"}
  ```

When you boil it down, there are really only three outcomes in the interaction between an app and an API:

- Everything worked—success.

- The application did something wrong—client error.

- The API did something wrong—server error.

Error Code

Start by using the following three codes which should map to the three outcomes earlier. If you need more, add them. But you shouldn't need to go beyond:

- 200: OK

- 400: Bad Request

- 500: Internal Server Error

If you're not comfortable reducing all your error conditions to these three, try picking among these additional five:

- 201: Created

- 304: Not Modified

- 404: Not Found

- 401: Unauthorized

- 403: Forbidden

Check out this good Wikipedia entry for all HTTP status codes: https://en.wikipedia.org/wiki/List_of_HTTP_status_codes.

Versioning

Never release an API without a version.

- Make the version mandatory.

- Specify the version with a "v" prefix. Move it all the way to the left in the URL so that it has the highest scope (e.g., /v1/dogs).

- Use a simple ordinal number. Don't use the dot notation like v1.2, because it implies a granularity of versioning that doesn't work well with APIs—it's an interface, not an implementation. Stick with v1, v2, and so on.

- How many versions should you maintain? Maintain at least one version back.

- For how long should you maintain a version? Give developers at least one cycle to react before obsoleting a version.

- There is a strong school of thought about putting format (xml or json) and version in the header. Simple rules we follow: If it changes the logic you write to handle the response, put it in the URL so you can see it easily. If it doesn't change the logic for each response (like OAuth information), put it in the header.

Partial Response

Partial response allows you to give developers just the information they need. Take, for example, a request for a tweet on the Twitter API. You'll get much more than a typical Twitter app often needs, including the name of the person, the text of the tweet, a timestamp, how often the message was retweeted, and a lot of metadata. Let's look at how several leading APIs handle giving developers just what they need in responses, including Google, who pioneered the idea of partial response:

- LinkedIn

  `/people:(id,first-name,last-name,industry)`This request on a person returns the ID, first name, last name, and the industry

- Facebook

  `/joe.smith/friends?fields=id,name,picture`

- Google

  `?fields=title,media`

Google and Facebook have a similar approach, which works well. They each have an optional parameter called "fields" after which you put the names of fields you want to be returned. As you can see in this example, you can also put subobjects in responses to pull in other information from additional resources.

Pagination

Make it easy for developers to paginate objects in a database. Let's look at how Facebook, Twitter, and LinkedIn handle pagination. Facebook uses offset and limit. Twitter uses page and rpp (records per page). LinkedIn uses start and count semantically. Facebook and LinkedIn do the same thing, that is, the LinkedIn start and count.

To get records 50 through 75 from each system, you would use the following:

- Facebook: `offset` 50 and `limit` 2

- Twitter: `page` 3 and `rpp` 25 (records per page)

- LinkedIn: `start` 50 and `count` 25

Multiple Formats

We recommend that you support more than one format—that you push things out in one format and accept as many formats as necessary. You can usually automate the mapping from format to format. Here's what the syntax looks like for a few key APIs:

- Google Data: `?alt=json`

- Foursquare: `/venue.json`

- LinkedIn: `Accept: application/json`

API Façade

Use the façade pattern when you want to provide a simple interface to a complex subsystem. Subsystems often get more complex as they evolve.

Implementing an API façade pattern involves three basic steps:

1. Design the ideal API—design the URLs, request parameters and responses, headers, query parameters, and so on. The API design should be self-consistent. This means you give the developers the information they need.

2. Implement the design with data stubs. This allows
    application developers to use your API and give
    you feedback even before your API is connected to
    internal systems.

3. Mediate or integrate between the façade and the
    systems.

API Solution Architecture

Developers and architects often think of APIs as a continuation of
the integration-based architectures that have long been in use within
enterprise IT. But this is a narrow view.

To understand the demands and requirements on APIs, let's discuss
typical solutions that are enabled by APIs.

Figure 4-5 shows the API solution architecture.

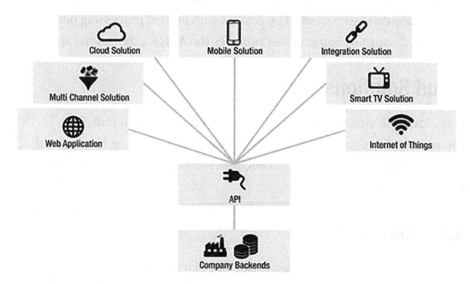

Figure 4-5. API solution architecture

API solutions typically consist of two components:

- Exposes the API

    - An exposed API resides on the server side, for example, in the cloud or on premise.

- Consumes the API

    - Web or mobile apps and embedded devices on IoT

Mobile Solutions

Mobile apps need to connect to the servers on the Internet to be usable at all or at least to be usable to their full potential—some business logic on the app and heavy-duty processing logic on servers in the cloud. Functionality hosted on these servers can be reached by API calls. Data captured on mobile devices is sent to servers by API calls, which hand the data to services and then to databases. Data delivered by APIs needs to be lightweight. This ensures APIs can be consumed by devices with limited processing power. Typically, the mobile app provider provides the APIs for the mobile app.

Cloud Solutions

SaaS cloud solutions typically consist of a web application and APIs. The web application is visible for the consumers. Under the hood, cloud solutions usually offer an API as well, for example, Dropbox, Salesforce, Workday, and Oracle Cloud.

Web Solutions

Web applications display dynamic web pages based upon user requests; web pages are created on the fly with data available from the back end. The web application pulls raw data from the APIs, processes the data (JSON, XML), and displays in HTML, for example, podcast or customer API.

Integration Solutions

APIs provide capabilities which are essential for connecting, extending the integrating software. By integrating software APIs, businesses can connect with other businesses. The business of an enterprise can be expanded by linking the business to a partner. Integration not only makes sense externally but also internally for integrating internal systems.

Multichannel Solutions

Today, an ecommerce system offers customers shopping on multiple platforms—mobile, web, tablet. It is required to provide a seamless experience when a consumer moves from one platform to another. This can be accomplished by providing a common API, which supports a multichannel maintaining state of user experience.

Smart TV Solutions

Smart TV offers not only TV channels, but provides interaction capabilities. These are all implemented by API calls to the servers.

Internet of Things

The Internet of Things is made up of physical devices with an Internet connection. The device connects to smart functions (e.g., sensors, scanners, etc.) which are exposed on the Internet via APIs.

Stakeholders in API Solutions

In API solutions, stakeholders are API providers, API consumers, and end users. We will discuss the roles of each here in this section.

API Providers

API providers develop, design, deploy, and manage APIs. API providers define the API portfolio, road map, and product mode. It is the responsibility of an API provider to decide which functionality is exposed by the API. In the solution-driven approach, only those APIs are built which are required by the consumer. In the top-down approach, API providers provide APIs which are good from an internal perspective, for example, from a reusability perspective.

API Consumers

Consumers need to know how to call an API and build an API client. API providers should provide a demo app to consume their API for the consumers.

End Users

End users do not call the API directly, but use the app developed by API consumers.

API Modeling

OpenAPI (Swagger)

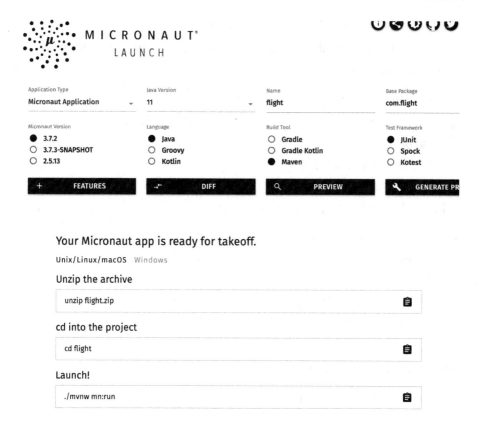

This tutorial walks you through the steps for creating OpenAPI specs using Swagger (Micronaut for a flight passenger API):

Import the flight folder in Visual Studio Code (VSC).

Create a model folder in VSC.

Create a controllers folder in VSC.

Create a service folder in VSC.

Create a Flight class in the model folder using VSC. Paste the following definition of the attributes of the Flight class and then select pasted code and using light bulb generate getter and setter methods.

Create a Passenger class in the model folder using VSC. Paste the passenger attributes' code and then generate getter and setter methods like for the flight object:

```
package com.rest.domain;
import io.swagger.v3.oas.annotations.media.Schema;
@Schema(description="Passenger")
public class Passenger {
 private String id;
 private String name;

 public String getId() {
       return id;
 }
 public void setId(String id) {
     this.id = id;
 }
 public String getName() {
       return name;
 }
 public void setName(String name) {
     this.name = name;
 }
}
```

Create a FlightService class in the service folder using VSC and paste the following folder. In this code, we are creating flightRepo for storing flights in memory. Get methods will be implemented to fetch details of a flight and list of all flights.

```
package com.rest.service;

import com.rest.domain.Flight;
import java.util.Map;
```

```java
import java.util.List;
import java.util.ArrayList;
import java.util.HashMap;
import java.util.concurrent.atomic.AtomicInteger;

public class FlightService {
static private Map<Integer, Flight> flightRepo = new
HashMap<Integer, Flight>();
static private AtomicInteger idCounter = new AtomicInteger();
public Flight getFlight(String id) {
    Flight flight = flightRepo.get(id);
    return flight;
}
public  List<Flight> getFlightsByPassenger(String
passengerId) {
    return new ArrayList<Flight>(flightRepo.values());
}
}
}
```

Create a PassengerService class in the service folder using VSC and paste the following code:

```java
package com.rest.service;

import com.rest.domain.Passenger;
import java.util.Map;
import java.util.List;
import java.util.ArrayList;
import java.util.HashMap;
import java.util.concurrent.atomic.AtomicInteger;

public class PassengerService {
static private Map<Integer, Passenger> passengerRepo = new
HashMap<Integer, Passenger>();
```

```
static private AtomicInteger idCounter = new AtomicInteger();
public Passenger getPassenger(int id) {
    Passenger passenger = passengerRepo.get(id);
    return passenger;
}
public  List<Passenger> getPassengers() {
    return new ArrayList<Passenger>(passengerRepo.values());
}
}
```

Create a FlightController class in the controller folder using VSC and paste the following code:

```
package com.rest.controller;

import com.rest.domain.Flight;
import com.rest.service.FlightService;
import io.micronaut.http.annotation.Get;
import io.micronaut.http.annotation.Controller;

import io.micronaut.http.HttpHeaders;
import io.micronaut.http.HttpResponse;
import io.micronaut.http.MediaType;
import io.micronaut.http.annotation.Produces;
import io.micronaut.http.annotation.Controller;
import io.micronaut.http.annotation.Delete;
import io.micronaut.http.annotation.Get;
import io.micronaut.http.annotation.Post;
import io.micronaut.http.annotation.Put;
import io.micronaut.http.annotation.Body;
import java.util.List;

@Controller("/flight")  // <2>
public class FlightController {
```

```
FlightService flightService;
public FlightController(FlightService flightService) { // <3>
    this.flightService = flightService;
}

  @Get("/{id}")
  public Flight getFlight(String id)     {
    Flight flight = flightService.getFlight(id);
    return flight;
  }
  @Get("/passenger/{id}")
  public List<Flight> getFlightsByPassenger(String id) {
    List<Flight> flights = flightService.
    getFlightsByPassenger(id);
    return flights;
  }
}
```

Create a PassengerController class in the controller folder using VSC and paste the following code:

```
package com.rest.controller;

import com.rest.domain.Passenger;
import com.rest.service.PassengerService;
import io.micronaut.http.annotation.Get;
import io.micronaut.http.annotation.Controller;

import io.micronaut.http.HttpHeaders;
import io.micronaut.http.HttpResponse;
import io.micronaut.http.MediaType;
import io.micronaut.http.annotation.Produces;
import io.micronaut.http.annotation.Controller;
```

```
import io.micronaut.http.annotation.Delete;
import io.micronaut.http.annotation.Get;
import io.micronaut.http.annotation.Post;
import io.micronaut.http.annotation.Put;
import io.micronaut.http.annotation.Body;
import java.util.List;

@Controller("/passenger")  // <2>
public class PassengerController {

  PassengerService passengerService;
  public PassengerController(PassengerService passengerService)
  { // <3>
      this.passengerService = passengerService;
  }

  @Get("/{id}")
  public Passenger getPassenger (int id)     {
    Passenger passenger = passengerService.getPassenger(id);
    return passenger;
  }
  @Get
  public List<Passenger> getPassengers() {
     List<Passenger> passengers = passengerService.
     getPassengers();
     return passengers;
  }
}
```

To get started, add Micronaut's openapi to the annotation processor scope of build configuration in the pom.xml file:

```
<path>
        <groupId>io.micronaut.openapi</groupId>
        <artifactId>micronaut-openapi</artifactId>
        <version>4.0.1</version>
</path>
```

For Swagger annotation, add the following to the pom.xml file:

```
<dependency>
    <groupId>io.swagger.core.v3</groupId>
    <artifactId>swagger-annotations</artifactId>
</dependency>
```

Once dependencies have been configured, the minimum requirement is to add the following to the Application class:

```
import io.swagger.v3.oas.annotations.OpenAPIDefinition;
import io.swagger.v3.oas.annotations.info.Contact;
import io.swagger.v3.oas.annotations.info.Info;
import io.swagger.v3.oas.annotations.info.License;

@OpenAPIDefinition(
        info = @Info(
                title = "Flight",
                version = "0.1",
                description = "Flight API",
                license = @License(name = "Apache 2.0", url =
                "https://foo.bar"),
                contact = @Contact(url = "https://gigantic-
                server.com", name = "Fred", email = "Fred@
                gigagantic-server.com")
        ))
```

Compile application using command "mvn package".

cd target/classes/META-INF/swagger

Generated OpenAPI YAML in file flight-0.1.yml.

Once you have modeled API, you can generate a document which could be shared with API consumers. Swagger allows to make API access in the browser and more readable. Next, we will configure Swagger.

Configure the following in the application.yml file to enable Swagger. You could find the application.yml file in the src/main/resources folder:

```
micronaut:
    router:
        static-resources:
            swagger:
                paths: classpath:META-INF/swagger
                mapping: /swagger/**
```

With the preceding configuration in place, when you run your application you can access your Swagger documentation at http://localhost:8080/swagger/flight-0.1.yml.

Summary

In this chapter, we started with API design strategies and then looked into the API creation process and modeling. Best practices for REST API design are discussed, followed by the API solution architecture. We compared API Modeling tools and then developed an API for flight passenger using Micronaut.

CHAPTER 5

API Portfolio and Framework

Abstract

This chapter starts with the API portfolio architecture and then gets into the framework for API development. An overview of the API framework starting from the client to data is discussed, and then the focus is shifted to review the services layer with an exercise implementing the services layer.

API Portfolio Architecture

Usually, an organization does not have one API but several APIs. All the APIs in the portfolio need to be consistent with each other, reusable, discoverable, and customizable.

Requirements

API portfolio design is a concern for different API stakeholders. Both API consumers and producers have significant advantages over a properly designed API portfolio, and both parties formulate requirements for an API portfolio regarding consistency, reuse, customization, discoverability, and longevity.

Consistency

An API solution, such as a mobile app, may use several APIs from the portfolio, and the output of one API is the input of another. So consistency is required about data structures, representations, URIs, error messages, and behavior of the APIs. API consumers find it easier to work with if it behaves similar to the last one and delivers similar error messages.

Reuse

A consistent portfolio consists of many commonalities among the APIs. These commonalities can be factored out, shared, and reused. Reuse leads to a speedup in the development. By reusing common elements, the wheel is not reinvented each time an API is built. Instead, a common library of patterns and know-how is shared and reused. Reuse can be realized in several ways:

- Reuse of an API by several apps
- Reuse of an API by multiple APIs
- Reuse of parts of an API

APIs should not be developed for a specific consumer. APIs should always be used by several consumers, solutions, or projects.

Customization

There might be consumers who might have specific requirements from the APIs, if the consumers of APIs are not a homogenous group. In such a scenario, customizations are required to the APIs to meet a consumer's individual needs. This contradicts with reuse requirements, but both can be realized at the same time.

Discoverability

To expand the usage of APIs, it should be easy for the API consumer to find and discover all APIs in an API portfolio. An API portfolio design needs to ensure that APIs can be found and all the information necessary for proper usage is available.

Longevity

This means that important aspects of the API do not change and stay stable for a long time. What needs to be stable is the signature of the API, the client-facing interface. A change in signature will break the apps built by the API consumer. For example, with IoT on "h/w devices" it is not easy to change.

How Do We Enforce These Requirements— Governance?

An API initiative is often regarded as an innovation lab of an enterprise. Imposing governance can contradict innovation. So to manage these conflicting requirements, an API portfolio may be split in two portfolios. One portfolio is dedicated to innovation and experiment. This portfolio requires lightweight governance processes. Another portfolio is dedicated to stable, productive APIs, which are offered to external API consumers.

Consistency

Each enterprise may implement its own set of consistency rules. When consistency rules are defined, consistency checks can be realized as manual or automated. Lightweight consistency checks can be realized by manual quality checks or review by a colleague. A complementary approach is by automated code generation based upon API description.

Reuse

There are two types of building blocks that are offered by an API Platform like security, logging, and error handler. Any other functional commonality or reusable solution pattern can be realized as a composition of building blocks. You could have your "own" API or third-party APIs. Third-party APIs could be integrated in an API Platform by creating an API Proxy on its "own" platform. This helps the consumer with homogenous security. API Proxy and API Platform architectures are discussed in the next chapter.

Customization

An API consumer is interested in data formatting and data delivery. Data gathering is, however, no concern to the API consumer. So these could be separated into two parts: one API we call "utility API" covers the data gathering; the other API, which delivers data and formats to the consumer requirements, is called "consumer API." Utility APIs cannot be called directly by a consumer; only consumer APIs can call these.

Discoverability

This could be manual or automated. Manual: Discover by API catalog or yellow pages. Automated: SOAP based through UDDI and WSDL. REST: Limited with the OPTIONS verb of HTTP.

Change Management

From an innovation or business perspective, there are forces to publish APIs as early as possible. From an IT governance perspective, APIs are published as late as possible. In a compromise solution, APIs are published early but only to pilot consumers, with the expectation that there will be changes, and APIs will break the app. Changes are classified into three groups: backward compatible, forward compatible, and not compatible. Backward compatibility is given if the old client can interact with the new API (adding query, header, or form parameter as long as they are optional; adding new fields in JSON or XML as long as they are optional; adding endpoint, e.g., new REST resource; adding new operations to existing endpoints, e.g., in SOAP; adding optional fields to request interface; changing mandatory fields to optional fields in an existing API). Forward compatibility is given if a new client can interact with an old API. It's hard to achieve, and generally it is nice to have it.

- Incompatible changes: If a change in the API breaks the client, the change was incompatible.

- Removing: Renaming fields in data structures or parameters in a request or response.

- Changing URI: For example, hostname, port.

- Changing data structure: Making a field the child of some other. Adding a new mandatory field in a data structure.

API Framework

As we have discussed, there are multiple solutions to an API, for example, web applications, mobile applications, etc. Each of these solutions talks to an API which is implemented through a multilayered architecture using design patterns. A **design pattern** is a general reusable solution to a commonly occurring problem within a given context in software **design**. A **design pattern** is not a finished **design** that can be transformed directly into source or machine code.

As shown, the Figure 5-1 multilayer framework consists of the following:

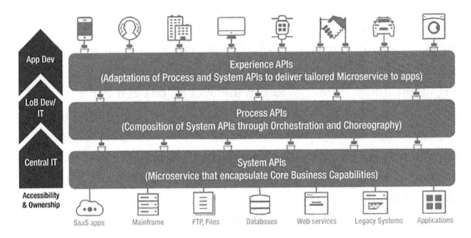

Figure 5-1. *API multilayered framework*

- Process APIs implemented by a services design pattern

- System APIs implemented by a data access object design pattern

- Experience APIs implemented by an API façade layer design pattern

Each layer is implemented using software engineering design patterns.

Process APIs: Services Layer

The services layer implements the business logic of the application: the reusable logic, process-specific logic, and the logic that interfaces with system APIs through orchestration and choreography. Orchestration (direct calls) in this sense is about aligning the line of business dev/IT request with the applications, data, and infrastructure. Choreography, in contrast, does not rely on a central coordinator. Rather, each API involved in the choreography knows exactly when to execute its operations and with whom to interact.

System APIs: Data Access Object

These system APIs or system-level services are in line with the concept of an autonomous service which has been designed with enough abstraction to hide the underlying systems of record, for example, databases, legacy systems, SaaS applications.

Typically, a data access object (DAO) is an object that provides an abstract interface to some type of database or other persistence mechanism. By mapping application calls to the persistence layer, DAO provides some specific data operations without exposing details of the system.

Experience APIs: API Façade

Both process and system APIs should be tailored and exposed to suit the needs of each business channel and digital touchpoint of solution architectures. The adaption is shaped by the desired digital experience and is what we call the experience API. This is implemented by API façade. The goal of an API façade pattern is to articulate internal systems and make them useful for the app developer providing a good APX (API experience).

Services Layer Implementation

The services layer implements the business logic of the application: the reusable logic, process-specific logic, and logic that interfaces with the legacy system. In the implementation of the services layer, a design pattern dependency injection is used. The general concept between dependency injections is called Inversion of Control. A class A has a dependency to class B if class A uses class B as a variable. If dependency injection is used, then the class B is given to class A via the constructor of the class A. This is then called "construction injection." If a setter is used, this is then called "setter injection."

A class should not configure itself but should be configured from outside. A design based on independent classes/components increases the reusability. A software design based on dependency injection is possible with standard Java. The Micronaut framework, which is used for the implementation in the exercises, just simplifies the use of dependency injection by providing a standard way of providing the configuration and by managing the reference to the created objects. The fundamental functionality provided by the Micronaut is dependency injection. Micronaut provides a lightweight container for dependency injection (DI). This container lets you inject required objects into other objects. This results in a design in which the Java classes are not hard-coupled.

FRAMEWORK: SERVICES

In the previous chapter, we implemented a flight passenger API for READ operations. This exercise uses a message domain object to implement CRUD (Create, Read, Update, and Delete) operations. The message domain object structure is pretty simple. There is an id, which identifies a message, and several other fields that we can see in the following JSON representation:

```
{ "id":1,
"message":"Welcome",
"from":"James",
"to":"John",
"creationDate":1388213547000
}
```

Pom.xml

Add the following to pom.xml:

```xml
<dependency>
    <groupId>javax.inject</groupId>
    <artifactId>javax.inject</artifactId>
    <version>1</version>
</dependency>
```

Message

Here is a POJO defining properties of the message:

```java
package com.rest.model;
public class Message {
 private int id;
 private String message;
 private String from;
 private String to;
 private String creationDate;

 public String getMessage() {
        return message;
 }
 public void setMessage(String message) {
     this.message = message;
 }
 public String getFrom() {
        return from;
 }
 public void setFrom(String from) {
     this.from = from;
 }
 public String getTo() {
        return to;
```

```
    }
    public void setTo(String to) {
        this.to = to;
    }
    public String getCreationDate() {
            return creationDate;
    }
    public void setCreationDate(String creationDate) {
        this.creationDate = creationDate;
    }
    public int getId() {
            return id;
    }
    public void setId(int id) {
        this.id = id;
    }
}
```

MessageController

In the message controller, we have CRUD operations for the message:

```
package com.rest.controller;

import com.rest.model.Message;
import com.rest.service.MessageService;
import io.micronaut.http.annotation.Get;
import io.micronaut.http.annotation.Controller;

import io.micronaut.http.HttpHeaders;
import io.micronaut.http.HttpResponse;
import io.micronaut.http.MediaType;
import io.micronaut.http.annotation.Produces;
import io.micronaut.http.annotation.Controller;
import io.micronaut.http.annotation.Delete;
import io.micronaut.http.annotation.Get;
```

```
import io.micronaut.http.annotation.Post;
import io.micronaut.http.annotation.Put;
import io.micronaut.http.annotation.Body;
import java.util.List;

@Controller("/message")   // <2>
public class MessageController {

  MessageService messageService;
  public MessageController(MessageService messageService)
{ // <3>
      this.messageService = messageService;
  }
  @Produces(MediaType.TEXT_XML)
  @Get("/xml")
    public HttpResponse<?> messageXml() {
        Message message = new Message();
        message.setMessage("Hello from Micronaut");
        final String xml = encodeAsXml(message);
        return HttpResponse.ok(xml).contentType(MediaType.
        APPLICATION_XML_TYPE);
    }
  @Produces(MediaType.TEXT_JSON)
  @Get("/json")
    public Message messageJson() {
        Message message = new Message();
        message.setMessage("Hello from Micronaut");
        return message;
    }
    private String encodeAsXml(final Message message) {
        return String.format("<message>%s</message>", message.
        getMessage());
    }

    @Post
```

```java
    public Message createMessage(@Body Message message) {
       messageService.createMessage(message);
       return message;
    }

  @Get("/{id}")
  public Message getMessage (int id)     {
    Message message = messageService.getMessage(id);
    return message;
  }
  @Get
  public List<Message> getMessages() {
     List<Message> messages = messageService.getMessages();
     return messages;
  }
  @Put("/{id}")
  public void updateMessage (int id, @Body Message update) {
     messageService.updateMessage(id, update);
  }
  @Delete("/{id}")
  public void deleteMessage(int id) {
     messageService.deleteMessage(id);
  }
}
```

MessageService

All the methods for CRUD (Create, Read, Update, and Delete) operations which have operations in memory of messages are moved here:

```java
package com.rest.service;

import com.rest.model.Message;
import java.util.Map;
import java.util.List;
```

```java
import java.util.ArrayList;
import java.util.HashMap;
import java.util.concurrent.atomic.AtomicInteger;
Import javax.inject.Singleton;
@Singleton
public class MessageService {
static private Map<Integer, Message> messageRepo = new
HashMap<Integer, Message>();
static private AtomicInteger idCounter = new AtomicInteger();
public Message getMessage(int id) {
        Message message = messageRepo.get(id);
        return message;
}
// add message
public void createMessage(Message message) {
        message.setId(idCounter.incrementAndGet());
        messageRepo.put(message.getId(), message);
}
// update message
public void updateMessage(int id, Message update) {
        Message current = messageRepo.get(id);
        current.setMessage(update.getMessage());
        current.setFrom(update.getFrom());
        current.setTo(update.getTo());
        current.setCreationDate(update.getCreationDate());
        messageRepo.put(current.getId(), current);
}
// Delete message
public void deleteMessage(int id) {
        Message current = messageRepo.remove(id);
}
public  List<Message> getMessages() {
    return new ArrayList<Message>(messageRepo.values());
}
```

API Tests(Curl)

```
curl -d '{ "id":1, "message":"test", "from":"test", "to":"test",
"creationDate":"12/12//2012" }' -H 'Content-Type: application/
json' http://localhost:8080/message
```

```
{"id":1,"message":"test","from":"test","to":"test","
creationDate":"12/12//2012"}
        curl -d '{ "id":2, "message":"test2", "from":"test",
        "to":"test", "creationDate":"12/12//2012" }' -H
        'Content-Type: application/json' http://localhost:
        8080/message
```

```
{"id":2,"message":"test2","from":"test","to":"test","creation
Date":"12/12//2012"}
 curl http://localhost:8080/message
```

```
[{"id":1,"message":"test","from":"test","to":"test",
"creationDate":"12/12//2012"},{"id":2,"message":"test2",
"from":"test","to":"test","creationDate":"12/12//2012}
```

```
curl http://localhost:8080/message/1
```

```
{"id":1,"message":"test","from":"test","to":"test",
"creationDate":"12/12//2012"}
            curl http://localhost:8080/message/2
{"id":2,"message":"test2","from":"test","to":"test",
"creationDate":"12/12//2012"}
```

```
curl -X "DELETE" http://localhost:8080/message/2
```

```
curl http://localhost:8080/message/2
{"message":"Not Found","_links":{"self":{"href":"/message/2",
"templated":false}},"_embedded":{"errors":[{"message":"Page Not
Found"}]}}
            curl http://localhost:8080/message
[{"id":1,"message":"test","from":"test","to":"test",
"creationDate":"12/12//2012"}]
```

Summary

Now we have two APIs in our portfolio: one is for the messaging, and the other for flight passengers. The flight status API implements the relationship of two objects Flight and Passenger, whereas the message service allows the creation and deletion of messages in addition to read. It is important to follow the same design for both the APIs.

CHAPTER 6

API Platform and Data Handler

Abstract

This chapter starts with API Platform architecture and then gets into the data handler pattern for the integration of RESTful APIs with actual data sources within an enterprise to make it more meaningful to the consumers through APIs.

API Platform Architecture

API Platforms are used by API providers to realize APIs efficiently. We will review the following:

- Why do we need an API Platform?

- What is an API Platform?

- Which capabilities does an API Platform have?

- How is an API Platform organized? What is the architecture of the API Platform?

- How does the API architecture fit in the surrounding technical architecture of an enterprise?

Why Do We Need an API Platform?

It is certainly technically feasible to build APIs without any platform or framework. But why would you? For a moment, let's think about databases, which provide a platform for building applications. You could certainly build your application without a database and write your own data storage library. But we typically do not do that. We use an existing database as a platform. And this is the best practice for good reasons. It allows us to focus on building an application that serves the business case, because we can reuse existing, proven components and build the application quicker. The same augmentation applies to API Platforms: API Platforms allow us to focus on building APIs that consumers love, since we can reuse existing, proven API building blocks and build APIs quicker.

So What Is an API Platform?

An API Platform consists of one of the following three components:

- API development platform

  - It offers tools to design and develop APIs quicker.

  - It offers building blocks, which are proven, reusable, and configurable.

- API runtime platform

  - This primarily executes APIs.

  - It serves API responses for incoming API requests of the consumers with nonfunctional properties like high throughput and low latency.

- API engagement platform

    - This platform allows API providers to manage their interaction with API consumers. It offers API documentation, credentials, and rate plans for the consumers.

So Which Capabilities Does the API Platform Have?

The following are the capabilities offered by the three components of the API Platform.

API Development Platform

The API development platform offers a toolbox for API design and development targeted for API developers who work for API providers. The toolbox contains API building blocks, which are proven, reusable, and configurable. When building APIs, certain functionality is needed over and over again. This can be accomplished by building blocks. Building blocks can be reused. Building blocks are tested so bugs are not there, and these are configurable so they can be adopted for many purposes. The building blocks offered by the API development platform span the following features at the minimum:

- Processing of HTTP requests and responses

- Header

- Query

- HTTP: Status code

- Methods

- Security: IP-based access limitation, location-based access limitation, time-based access limitation, front-end authentication and authorization, OAuth, basic authorization, API key, back-end authentication and authorization (with LDAP, SAML)

- Front-end protocols: HTTP (REST), SOAP, RPC, RMI

- Data format transformation: XML to JSON and JSON to XML

- Structural transformation: XLST, XPATH

- Data integrity and protection: Encryption

- Routing to one or more back ends

- Aggregation of multiple APIs and/or multiple back ends

- Throttling to protect back-end rate limitation and throughput limitation

- Load balancing for incoming requests to the API Platform and outgoing requests to the back ends

- Hooks for logging

- Hooks for analytics

- Monetization capabilities

- Language for implementing APIs: Java, JavaScript, etc. (Jersey, Restlet, Spring)

- IDE for API development with editor, debugger, and deployment tools: Eclipse, JDeveloper, NetBeans

- Language for designing APIs: YAML, RAML, etc.

- Design tools for creating API interface designs: RAML, Swagger, Blueprint

- Tools for generating documentation and API code skeletons based upon design: RAML, Swagger

API Runtime Platform

The API runtime platform primarily executes APIs. It enables the APIs to accept incoming requests from API consumers and serve responses.

- It should deliver nonfunctional properties like

  - High availability, high security, high throughput

  - To meet these properties, the platform offers

    - Load balancing

    - Connection pooling

    - Caching

- It should also offer capabilities for monitoring of APIs, logging, and analytics to check desired nonfunctional properties are met.

API Engagement Platform

The API engagement platform is used by API providers to interact with its community of API consumers. API providers use the following capabilities of the API engagement platform:

- API management: Configuration and reconfiguration of APIs without the need for deployment

- API discovery: A mechanism for clients to obtain information about APIs

- Consumer onboarding: App key generation, API Console

- Community management: Blogs

- Documentation

- Version management

- Management of monetization and service-level SLAs

API consumers use the engagement platform for

- Overview of an API portfolio

- Documentation of APIs

- Possibility of trying APIs interactively

- Example source code for integration

  - Self-service to get access to APIs

  - Client tooling, such as code generation for clients

How Is an API Platform Organized? What Is the Architecture of the API Platform?

Usually, APIs are not only deployed on the production system, but need to be deployed on different stages of increasing maturity. The stages are also sometimes called environments. Each of the stages has a specific purpose and is separated from the other stages to isolate potential errors:

- Simulation: Used for playing with interface design, provides mocks or simulation of an API

- Development: Used for development, which will eventually go to production

- Testing: Used for manual black box testing and integration testing

- Preproduction: Used as a practice for production and for acceptance testing

- Production: Used as a real system for consumers

As shown in Figure 6-1, the API development platform is used for design and development. The API runtime platform is used for deployment. The API engagement platform is used for publishing the API.

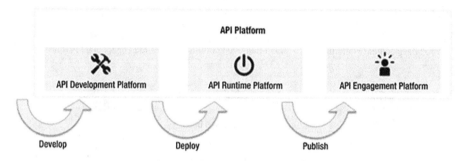

Figure 6-1. *API Platform architecture*

How Does the API Architecture Fit in the Surrounding Technical Architecture of an Enterprise?

An API Platform is not isolated, but it needs to be integrated in existing architecture in the enterprise. Firewall is used to improve security. Load balancers are used to improve performance and are usually placed between the Internet and the API Platform. IAM (Identity and Access Management) systems are for managing identity information and LDAP or Active Directory as shown in Figure 6-2.

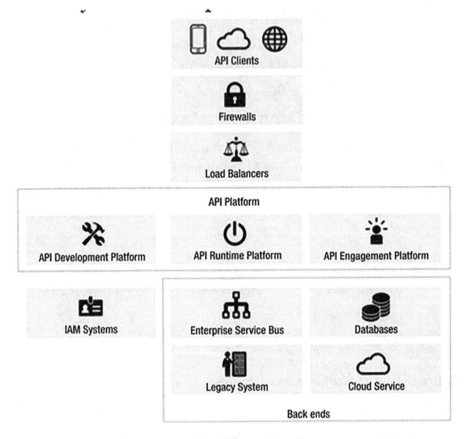

Figure 6-2. *API architecture in an enterprise*

Back-end systems for providing the core functionality of the enterprise: Back ends may be databases, applications, enterprise service buses, web services using SOAP, message queues, and REST services.

Data Handler

As mentioned in the previous section, we use an existing database as a platform. A data handler, a data access object (DAO), and a command query responsibility segregation (CQRS) all provide an abstract interface to some type of database or any other persistence mechanism. A data handler is a layer which handles data in the framework. A data access object is a design pattern used to implement the access from the database inside the data handler. The CQRS pattern, on the other hand, provides a mechanism to segment query and transactional data in the data handler.

Data Access Object

By mapping application calls to the persistence layer, a DAO provides some specific data operations without exposing details of the database. The advantage of using data access objects is the relative simplicity, and it provides separation between two important parts of an application that can but should not know anything about each other and which can be expected to evolve frequently and independently. Changing business logic can rely on the same DAO interface, while changes to persistence logic do not affect DAO clients as long as the interface remains correctly implemented. All details of storage are hidden from the rest of the application (see information hiding). Thus, possible changes to the persistence mechanism can be implemented by just modifying one DAO implementation while the rest of the application isn't affected. DAOs act as an intermediary between the application and the database. DAOs move data back and forth between objects and database records.

For accessing databases, there are different APIs available (e.g., JPA, which will be used in the class lab).

Command Query Responsibility Segregation (CQRS)

New demands are being put on IT organizations every day to deliver agile, high-performance integrated mobile and web applications. In the meantime, the technology landscape is getting complex every day with the advent of new technologies like REST, NoSQL, and the cloud, while existing technologies like SOAP and SQL still rule everyday work. Rather than taking a religious side of the debate, NoSQL can successfully coexist with SQL in this "polyglot" of data storage and formats. However, this integration also adds another layer of complexity both in architecture and implementation. We will talk about the following.

SQL Development Process

The application development life cycle means changes to the database schema first, followed by the bindings, then internal schema mapping, and finally the SOAP or JSON services, and eventually the client code. This all costs the project time and money. It also means that the "code" (pick your language here) and the business logic would also need to be modified to handle the changes to the model. Figure 6-3 shows the traditional CRUD architecture.

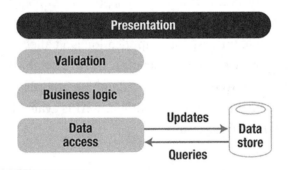

Figure 6-3. Traditional CRUD architecture

NoSQL Process

NoSQL is gaining supporters among many SQL shops for various reasons, including low cost, the ability to handle unstructured data, scalability, and performance. The first thing database folks notice is that there is no schema. These document-style storage engines can handle huge volumes of structured, semistructured, and unstructured data. The very nature of schemaless documents allows change to a document structure without having to go through the formal change management process (or data architect).

Do I Have to Choose Between SQL and NoSQL?

The bottom line is both have their place and are suited for certain types of data—SQL for structured data and NoSQL for unstructured data. NoSQL databases are more scalable than SQL databases. So why not have the capability to mix and match this data depending on the application? This can be done by creating a single REST API across both SQL and NoSQL databases.

Why a Single REST API?

The answer is simple—the new agile and mobile world demands this "mash-up" of data into a document-style JSON response.

Martin Fowler described the pattern called "CQRS" that is more relevant today in a "polyglot" of servers, data, services, and connections (Figure 6-4).

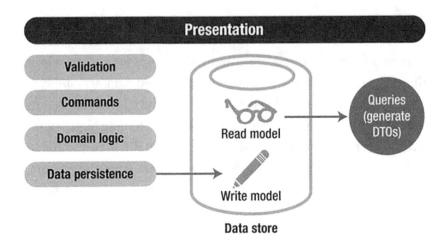

Figure 6-4. *Basic CQRS architecture*

In this design pattern, the REST API requests (GET) return documents from multiple sources (e.g., mash-ups). In the update process, the data is subject to business logic derivations, validations, event processing, and database transactions. This data may then be pushed back into the NoSQL using asynchronous events. The advantage of NoSQL databases over SQL for this purpose is that NoSQL has dynamic schema for unstructured data. Also, NoSQL databases are horizontally scalable, which means NoSQL databases are scaled by increasing the database servers in the pool of resources to reduce the load, whereas SQL databases are scaled by increasing horsepower of the server where the database is hosted. Figure 6-5 shows the CQRS architecture with separate read and write stores. When you have a requirement of very, very large data volumes, you would choose separate stores.

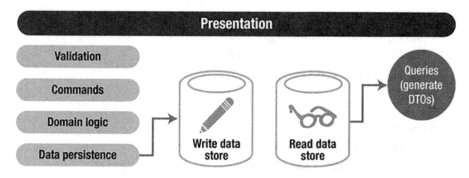

Figure 6-5. *CQRS architecture with separate read and write stores*

FRAMEWORK: DATA HANDLER

This exercise will implement a data handler or data access object for the quote domain object using the Java Persistence API (JPA). JPA is a Java specification for accessing, persisting, and managing data between Java objects/classes and a relational database. We will use our domain object message and implement CRUD operations using JPA in DAO.

Pom.xml

Update pom.xml with the following dependencies:

```xml
<?xml version="1.0" encoding="UTF-8"?>
<project xmlns="http://maven.apache.org/POM/4.0.0"
xmlns:xsi="http://www.w3.org/2001/XMLSchema-instance"
        xsi:schemaLocation="http://maven.apache.org/POM/4.0.0
http://maven.apache.org/xsd/maven-4.0.0.xsd">
  <modelVersion>4.0.0</modelVersion>
  <groupId>com.rest</groupId>
  <artifactId>quote</artifactId>
  <version>0.1</version>
  <packaging>${packaging}</packaging>
```

```
<parent>
  <groupId>io.micronaut</groupId>
  <artifactId>micronaut-parent</artifactId>
  <version>3.4.3</version>
</parent>

<properties>
  <packaging>jar</packaging>
  <jdk.version>11</jdk.version>
  <micronaut.version>3.4.3</micronaut.version>
  <micronaut.data.version>3.3.0</micronaut.data.version>
  <exec.mainClass>com.rest.Application</exec.mainClass>
  <micronaut.runtime>netty</micronaut.runtime>
</properties>

<repositories>
  <repository>
    <id>central</id>
    <url>https://repo.maven.apache.org/maven2</url>
  </repository>
</repositories>
<dependencies>
    <dependency>
      <groupId>io.micronaut</groupId>
      <artifactId>micronaut-inject</artifactId>
      <scope>compile</scope>
    </dependency>
    <dependency>
      <groupId>io.micronaut</groupId>
      <artifactId>micronaut-validation</artifactId>
      <scope>compile</scope>
    </dependency>
    <dependency>
```

```
      <groupId>org.junit.jupiter</groupId>
      <artifactId>junit-jupiter-api</artifactId>
      <scope>test</scope>
    </dependency>
    <dependency>
      <groupId>org.junit.jupiter</groupId>
      <artifactId>junit-jupiter-engine</artifactId>
      <scope>test</scope>
    </dependency>
    <dependency>
      <groupId>io.micronaut.test</groupId>
      <artifactId>micronaut-test-junit5</artifactId>
      <scope>test</scope>
    </dependency>
    <dependency>
      <groupId>io.micronaut</groupId>
      <artifactId>micronaut-http-client</artifactId>
      <scope>compile</scope>
    </dependency>
    <dependency>
      <groupId>io.micronaut</groupId>
      <artifactId>micronaut-http-server-netty</artifactId>
      <scope>compile</scope>
    </dependency>
    <dependency>
      <groupId>io.micronaut</groupId>
      <artifactId>micronaut-jackson-databind</artifactId>
      <scope>compile</scope>
    </dependency>
    <dependency>
<groupId>io.micronaut</groupId>
      <artifactId>micronaut-http-server-netty</artifactId>
      <scope>compile</scope>
    </dependency>
```

```xml
<dependency>
  <groupId>io.micronaut</groupId>
  <artifactId>micronaut-jackson-databind</artifactId>
  <scope>compile</scope>
</dependency>
<dependency>
  <groupId>io.micronaut</groupId>
  <artifactId>micronaut-runtime</artifactId>
  <scope>compile</scope>
</dependency>
<dependency>
  <groupId>io.micronaut.data</groupId>
  <artifactId>micronaut-data-jdbc</artifactId>
  <scope>compile</scope>
</dependency>
<dependency>
  <groupId>io.micronaut.reactor</groupId>
  <artifactId>micronaut-reactor</artifactId>
  <scope>compile</scope>
</dependency>
<dependency>
  <groupId>mysql</groupId>
  <artifactId>mysql-connector-java</artifactId>
</dependency>
<dependency>
  <groupId>io.micronaut.reactor</groupId>
  <artifactId>micronaut-reactor-http-client</artifactId>
  <scope>compile</scope>
</dependency>
<dependency>
  <groupId>io.micronaut.sql</groupId>
  <artifactId>micronaut-jdbc-hikari</artifactId>
  <scope>compile</scope>
</dependency>
```

```xml
  <dependency>
   <groupId>io.micronaut.data</groupId>
   <artifactId>micronaut-data-hibernate-jpa</artifactId>
  </dependency>
  <dependency>
   <groupId>io.micronaut.sql</groupId>
   <artifactId>micronaut-hibernate-jpa</artifactId>
  </dependency>
   <dependency>
   <groupId>io.swagger.core.v3</groupId>
   <artifactId>swagger-annotations</artifactId>
  </dependency>
  <dependency>
     <groupId>jakarta.annotation</groupId>
     <artifactId>jakarta.annotation-api</artifactId>
     <scope>compile</scope>
  </dependency>
  <dependency>
     <groupId>ch.qos.logback</groupId>
     <artifactId>logback-classic</artifactId>
     <scope>runtime</scope>
  </dependency>
  <dependency>
     <groupId>com.h2database</groupId>
     <artifactId>h2</artifactId>
     <scope>runtime</scope>
  </dependency>
 </dependencies>
<build>
   <plugins>
     <plugin>
        <groupId>io.micronaut.build</groupId>
        <artifactId>micronaut-maven-plugin</artifactId>
     </plugin>
```

```xml
      <plugin>
        <groupId>org.apache.maven.plugins</groupId>
        <artifactId>maven-compiler-plugin</artifactId>
        <configuration>
          <!-- Uncomment to enable incremental compilation -->
          <!-- <useIncrementalCompilation>false</useIncremental
          Compilation> -->

          <annotationProcessorPaths combine.children="append">
            <path>
              <groupId>io.micronaut</groupId>
              <artifactId>micronaut-http-validation</artifactId>
              <version>${micronaut.version}</version>
            </path>
            <path>
              <groupId>io.micronaut.data</groupId>
              <artifactId>micronaut-data-processor</artifactId>
              <version>${micronaut.data.version}</version>
            </path>
          </annotationProcessorPaths>
          <compilerArgs>
            <arg>-Amicronaut.processing.group=com.rest</arg>
            <arg>-Amicronaut.processing.module=quote</arg>
          </compilerArgs>
        </configuration>
      </plugin>
    </plugins>
  </build>

</project>
```

Product

Here is a POJO defining properties of a product or catalog:

```java
package com.rest.domain;
import io.swagger.v3.oas.annotations.media.Schema;
import javax.persistence.*;
import javax.validation.constraints.Size;
@Schema(description="Product")
@Entity
public class Product {
 @Id
 @GeneratedValue(strategy = GenerationType.IDENTITY)
 @Column(name="ID")
 private Long id;

 @Column(name="NAME")
 @Size(max = 20)
 private String name;

 @Column(name="DESCRIPTION")
 @Size(max = 50)
 private String description;;

 @Column(name="CREATE_DATE")
 @Size(max = 40)
 private String createDate;;

 @Column(name="CHANGE_DATE")
 @Size(max = 40)
 private String changeDate;;

 @Column(name="UNIT_PRICE")
 @Size(max = 20)
 private float unitPrice;;
```

```java
@Column(name="CREATOR")
private String creator;

public Long getId() {
    return id;
}

public void setId(Long id) {
    this.id = id;
}

public String getName() {
    return name;
}
public void setName(String name) {
    this.name = name;
}

public String getDescription() {
    return description;
}

public void setDescription(String description) {
    this.description = description;
}

public String getCreateDate() {
    return createDate;
}

public void setCreateDate(String createDate) {
    this.createDate = createDate;
}

public String getChangeDate() {
    return changeDate;
}
```

```
public void setChangeDate(String changeDate) {
    this.changeDate = changeDate;
}

public float getUnitPrice() {
    return unitPrice;
}

public void setUnitPrice(float unitPrice) {
    this.unitPrice = unitPrice;
}

public String getCreator() {
    return creator;
}

public void setCreator(String creator) {
    this.creator = creator;
};
}
```

Quote

Here is quote POJO having quote properties with mapping to quote lines:

```
package com.rest.domain;
import io.swagger.v3.oas.annotations.media.Schema;
import javax.persistence.*;
import javax.validation.constraints.Size;
import java.util.List;
@Schema(description="Quote")
@Entity
public class Quote {

 @Id
 @GeneratedValue(strategy = GenerationType.IDENTITY)
 @Column(name="ID")
 private Long id;
```

117

```
@Column(name="CUSTOMER_ID")
private Long customerId;

@Column(name="QUOTE_DATE")
@Size(max = 50)
private String quoteDate;;

@Column(name="BILLING_ADDRESS")
@Size(max = 20)
private String billingAddress;

@Column(name="BILLING_CITY")
@Size(max = 20)
private String billingCity;;

@Column(name="BILLING_STATE")
@Size(max = 20)
private String billingState;;

@Column(name="BILLING_COUNTRY")
@Size(max = 20)
private String billingCountry;;

@Column(name="BILLING_POSTAL_CODE")
@Size(max = 20)
private String billingPostalCode;;

@Column(name="TOTAL")
@Size(max = 20)
private float total;
@OneToMany (fetch = FetchType.EAGER, cascade = CascadeType.ALL)
@JoinTable(name = "Quote_Line_Mapping",
joinColumns = @JoinColumn(name = "quote_id"),
inverseJoinColumns = @JoinColumn(name = "id"))
private List<QuoteLine> quoteLines;
```

```java
public void setQuoteLines(List<QuoteLine> quoteLines) {
    this.quoteLines = quoteLines;
}

public List<QuoteLine> getQuoteLines() {
    return quoteLines;
}

public Long getId() {
    return id;
}

public void setId(Long id) {
    this.id = id;
}

public Long getCustomerId() {
    return customerId;
}

public void setCustomerId(Long customerId) {
    this.customerId = customerId;
}

public String getQuoteDate() {
    return quoteDate;
}

public void setQuoteDate(String quoteDate) {
    this.quoteDate = quoteDate;
}

public String getBillingAddress() {
    return billingAddress;
}

public void setBillingAddress(String billingAddress) {
    this.billingAddress = billingAddress;
}
```

```java
    public String getBillingCity() {
        return billingCity;
    }

    public void setBillingCity(String billingCity) {
        this.billingCity = billingCity;
    }

    public String getBillingState() {
        return billingState;
    }

    public void setBillingState(String billingState) {
        this.billingState = billingState;
    }

    public String getBillingCountry() {
        return billingCountry;
    }

    public void setBillingCountry(String billingCountry) {
        this.billingCountry = billingCountry;
    }

    public String getBillingPostalCode() {
        return billingPostalCode;
    }

    public void setBillingPostalCode(String billingPostalCode) {
        this.billingPostalCode = billingPostalCode;
    }

    public float getTotal() {
        return total;
    }

    public void setTotal(float total) {
        this.total = total;
    };
```

QuoteLine

Here is quote line POJO with properties of the line item and mapping to the product:

```java
package com.rest.domain;
import io.swagger.v3.oas.annotations.media.Schema;
import javax.persistence.*;

@Schema(description="QuoteLine")
@Entity
public class QuoteLine {

  @Id
  @GeneratedValue(strategy = GenerationType.IDENTITY)
  @Column(name="ID")
  private Long id;

  @Column(name="QUOTE_ID")
  private Long quoteId;

@OneToOne(cascade = CascadeType.ALL)
@JoinColumn(name = "product_id", referencedColumnName = "id")
private Product product;

  @Column(name="UNIT_PRICE")
  private float unitPrice;

  @Column(name="QUANTITY")
  private Long  quantity;

public Product getProduct() {
    return product;
}

public void setProduct(Product product) {
    this.product = product;
}
```

```java
public Long getId() {
    return id;
}

public void setId(Long id) {
    this.id = id;
}
public void setId(Long id) {
    this.id = id;
}

public Long getQuoteId() {
    return quoteId;
}

public void setQuoteId(Long quoteId) {
    this.quoteId = quoteId;
}

public float getUnitPrice() {
    return unitPrice;
}

public void setUnitPrice(float unitPrice) {
    this.unitPrice = unitPrice;
}

public Long getQuantity() {
    return quantity;
}

public void setQuantity(Long quantity) {
    this.quantity = quantity;
};

}
```

Next, we will create repositories for product, quote, and quote line items for CRUD operations.

ProductRepo

```
package com.rest.repository;

import io.micronaut.data.annotation.Repository;
import io.micronaut.data.repository.CrudRepository;

import com.rest.domain.Product;

@Repository
public interface ProductRepo extends
CrudRepository<Product, Long> {
}
```

QuoteRepo

```
package com.rest.repository;

import io.micronaut.data.annotation.Repository;
import io.micronaut.data.repository.CrudRepository;

import com.rest.domain.Quote;

@Repository
public interface QuoteRepo extends CrudRepository<Quote, Long> {
}
```

QuoteLineRepo

```
package com.rest.repository;

import io.micronaut.data.annotation.Repository;
import io.micronaut.data.repository.CrudRepository;
```

```
import com.rest.domain.QuoteLine;;

@Repository
public interface QuoteLineRepo extends
CrudRepository<QuoteLine, Long> {
}
```

Next, we will create a quote controller implementing Get, Post, Put, and Delete endpoints for the quote API.

QuoteController

```
package com.rest.controller;

import com.rest.domain.Quote;
import com.rest.repository.QuoteRepo;
import io.micronaut.http.annotation.Get;
import io.micronaut.http.annotation.Controller;
import io.micronaut.http.annotation.Delete;
import io.micronaut.http.annotation.Post;
import io.micronaut.http.annotation.Put;
import io.micronaut.http.annotation.Body;
import java.util.List;
import java.util.ArrayList;
@Controller("/quote")  // <2>
public class QuoteController {

  QuoteRepo quoteRepo;
  public QuoteController(QuoteRepo quoteRepo) { // <3>
      this.quoteRepo = quoteRepo;
  }
```

```
@Post
public Quote createQuote(@Body Quote quote) {
    return quoteRepo.save(quote);
}

@Get("/{id}")
public Quote getQuote (Long id)     {
   Quote quote = quoteRepo.findById(id).get();
   return quote;
 }
 @Get
 public List<Quote> getQuotes() {
    Iterable<Quote> quotes =  quoteRepo.findAll();
    List<Quote> result = new ArrayList<Quote>();
    quotes.forEach(result::add);
    return result;
}
@Put("/{id}")
public void updateQuote (Long id, Quote update) {
   Quote quote = quoteRepo.findById(id).get();
   quoteRepo.delete(quote);
   quoteRepo.save(update);
}
@Delete("/{id}")
public void deleteQuote(Long id) {
   Quote quote = quoteRepo.findById(id).get();
   quoteRepo.delete(quote);
}

}
```

Creating quote

```
curl -d '{  "customerId":"123", "quoteDate":"11/07/2022",
"billingAddress":"722 Main St", "billingCity":"San
Jose", "billingState": "CA", "billingCountry":
"USA", "billingPostalCode": "95035", "total" :
123, "quoteLines" : [{"quoteId" : 1, "product" :
{"name":"test", "description":"test", "createDate":"test",
"changeDate":"12/12//2012", "unitPrice": 1.0, "creator": "creat"
}, "unitPrice": 12, "quantity" : 1}]}' -H 'Content-Type:
application/json' http://localhost:8080/quote
```

Reading quote

```
curl http://localhost:8080/quote/1
```

Summary

In this chapter, we started with the API Platform architecture and then got into the data handler pattern for the integration of RESTful APIs with actual data sources. In the exercise, we demonstrated the implementation of a data handler using JPA.

CHAPTER 7

API Management and CORS

Abstract

In this chapter, we will start with façade and review API management requirements/solutions available.

Façade

In this section, we will first review the façade design pattern, and then in the second part, we will get into details about how façade is applied to the APIs.

Façade Pattern

Before we discuss the façade pattern, let's consider what a façade is in the real world. The most obvious example is that of buildings, which all have an exterior to protect and decorate, hiding the internal workings of the interior. This exterior is the façade.

S. Patni, *Pro RESTful APIs with Micronaut*, https://doi.org/10.1007/978-1-4842-9200-6_7

127

Now we can get closer to APIs by considering operating systems. Just like in buildings, an operating system provides an exterior shell to the interior functionality of a computer. This simplified interface makes an OS easier to use and protects the core from clumsy users.

This is where the definition of the façade pattern in On Design Patterns comes in handy:

> Provide a unified interface to a set of interfaces in a subsystem. Façade defines a higher-level interface that makes the subsystem easier to use.

Consider Figure 7-1; you can see how the façade pattern puts an intermediate layer between the packages of the application and any client that wants to interact with them.

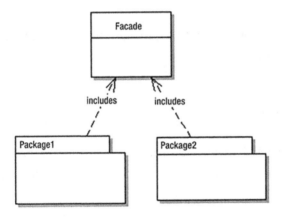

Figure 7-1. *Façade pattern*

API Façade

Like all implementations of the façade pattern, an API façade is a simple interface to a complex problem. Figure 7-2 shows internal subsystems in an enterprise. As shown, each internal subsystem is complex in itself: for example, JDBC hides the inner workings of database connectivity.

Figure 7-2. *Internal subsystems*

Figure 7-3 shows an API façade layer on the top of internal subsystems of the enterprise, providing a unified interface to apps.

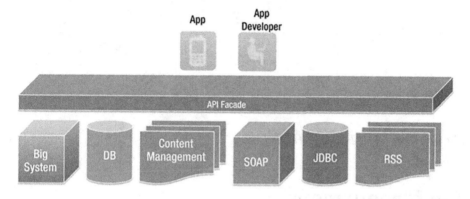

Figure 7-3. *API Façade - High Level*

Implementing an API façade pattern involves three basic steps:

- Design the API: Identify the URLs, request parameters and responses, payloads, headers, query parameters, and so on.

- Implement the design with mock data. App developers can then test the API before the API is connected to internal subsystems, with all the complications that entail.

- Connect the façade with the internal systems to create the live API.

Figure 7-4 shows these layers.

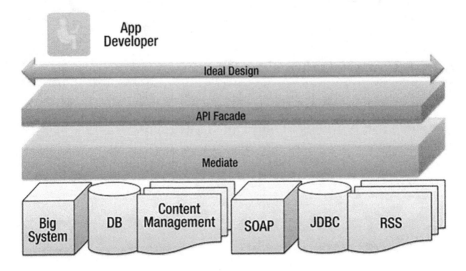

Figure 7-4. *API Façade-High Level*

API Management

An API management tool provides the means to expose your API to external developers in an easy and affordable manner.

Here are the features of an API management service:

- Documentation

- Analytics and statistics

- Deployment

- Developer engagement

- Sandbox environment

- Traffic management and caching abilities

- Security

- Availability

- Monetization

- API life cycle management

- API management vendors implement their solution in three different ways:

  - Proxy: All traffic goes through the API management tool, which is placed as a layer between the application and users.

  - Agents: These are plug-ins for servers. They do not intercept API calls like proxies.

  - Hybrid: This approach picks features of proxies and agents and integrates them. You can then pick which features you need.

API Life Cycle

The default API life cycle has the following stages:

- Analysis: The API is analyzed, and mock responses are created for a limited set of consumers to try out the API and provide feedback. It's also analyzed for monetization, as discussed in the following section.

- Being created/development: The API is being created: designed, developed, and secured. The API metadata is saved, but it is not visible yet nor deployed.

- Published/operations: The API is visible and eventually published and is now in the maintenance stage, where it is scaled and monitored.

In addition, there are two more stages:

- Deprecated: The API is still deployed (available at runtime to existing users), but is not visible to new users. An API is automatically deprecated when a new version is published.

- Retired: The API is unpublished and deleted.

These are discussed in the next section.

Figure 7-5 shows an API life cycle.

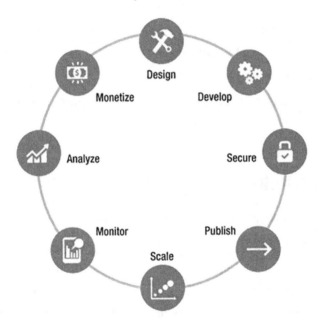

Figure 7-5. *API life cycle*

API Retirement

As old age comes, we get to retire, and the same is true with APIs. With time and due to the following reasons, an API is retired or deprecated:

- Lack of partner or third-party developer innovation

- Losing market share due to exposure of data by APIs

- Changes in the technology stack, for example, REST replacing SOAP

- Security concern: Making public APIs private due to security requirement of the information or data exposed by APIs

- Versioning: Most common reason due to functionality changes

Some of the examples of API retirement are Netflix, Google Earth, Twitter V1.0, etc.

API Monetization

Digital assets or services provide real value to customers, partners, and end users, and hence they should be a source of revenue for your company, as well as an important part of your business model.

There are three business models for monetizing APIs:

- The revenue share model, where the API consumer gets paid for the incremental business they trigger for the API provider.

- The fee-based model, where the API consumer pays the provider for API usage.

- The third and final business model is freemium. Freemium models can be based on a variety of factors such as volume, time, or some combination; they can be implemented as stand-alone or hybrid models (in conjunction with the revenue share or fee-based).

Cross-Origin Resource Sharing (CORS)

"Cross-Origin Resource Sharing" (CORS) is a mechanism that allows TypeScript or JavaScript on a web page to make XMLHttpRequests to another domain, not the domain the JavaScript originated from. Such "cross-domain" requests would otherwise be forbidden by web browsers, per the same origin security policy. CORS defines a way in which the browser and the server can interact to determine whether or not to allow the cross-origin request. It is more useful than only allowing same-origin requests, but it is more secure than simply allowing all such cross-origin requests. The Cross-Origin Resource Sharing standard works by adding new HTTP headers that allow servers to describe the set of origins that are permitted to read that information using a web browser.

How to implement CORS? For example:

```
return Response.ok() //200
.entity(quote)
.header("Access-Control-Allow-Origin", "*")
.header("Access-Control-Allow-Methods", "GET, POST,
DELETE, PUT").
allow("OPTIONS").build();
```

Summary

In this chapter, we reviewed API management requirements/solutions and discussed Cross-Origin Resource Sharing (CORS) to support client implementation.

Index

A

Agile design strategy, 53
Agility, 53
API consumers, 72, 80
API development platform, 98
    features, 99–101
    toolbox, 99
API engagement platform, 99,
      101, 102
API façade, 68, 69, 87, 128–130
API life cycle, 132
    analysis, 131
    being created/
      development, 131
    deprecated, 132
    published/operations, 131
    retired, 132
API management, 130, 131
API modeling, 58–61, 72
API monetization, 133
API multilayered framework
    API façade, 87
    components, 86
    data access object, 87
    services layer, 86
API platforms, 84
    API engagement, 101, 102
    API providers, 97

architecture, 97, 126
components, 98, 99
CQRS, 106
data access object, 105
data handler, 105
development platform, 99–101
importance, 98
NoSQL process, 107
organizations, 102, 103
SQL development
      process, 106
SQL *vs.* NoSQL process, 107
technical architecture, 103, 104
API portfolio, 57
    change management, 85
    consistency, 82, 84
    customization, 83, 84
    discoverability, 83, 84
    longevity, 83
    message, 25
    online flight, 24
    requirements, 82, 83
    reuse, 82, 84
API providers, 72, 97, 101
API Proxy, 84
API retirement, 132, 133
API Runtime Platform, 98, 101, 103
APIs implementation, 42, 44–48

V

W

X, Y, Z

Printed in the United States
by Baker & Taylor Publisher Services